Considerations

Considerations

✦

Emails From the Heart

Ron Jordan

Edited with the assistance of
Gail Taylor

iUniverse, Inc.
New York Lincoln Shanghai

Considerations
Emails From the Heart

iUniverse, Inc.

For information address:
iUniverse, Inc.
2021 Pine Lake Road, Suite 100
Lincoln, NE 68512
www.iuniverse.com

ISBN: 0-595-28346-2 (pbk)
ISBN: 0-595-74785-X (cloth)

Printed in the United States of America

For Mother…

Who taught me the Joy of reading,

and the "Art" of expression.

Contents

Preface

I had no intention of writing a book. It was only because of dear friends and family that I even contemplated the possibility. Their occasional remarks that, "You should write a book!" gave the idea some credibility. I don't consider myself an "Author"—but a "Storyteller". Authors are educated people well-versed in the book-making business. I don't make pretensions about being something I'm not. I enjoy sharing my thoughts with others, and people sharing their thoughts with me. Progressing through a personal and turbulent period of time, I decided to share with others about what was going on in my life. I did this through emails, and I called those emails my *Considerations*.

The drawback is that "honesty" sometimes hurts the very people you care about the most. I stepped on a few toes in writing those emails and hurt some people's feelings—my own as well, in the process. To those whom I have offended, I offer my sincerest apologies. Then there were other people who were continually supportive during this period of time and who I somehow missed with all of those "darts" that I was throwing around. How in the world did I miss you?

There are so many individuals who have become a part of my life during this writing process. Usually an "Author" will list the names of those people that deserve personal thanks in the *Preface* portion of the book—but I'm not an Author, I am a Storyteller. Instead, I have expressed my thanks to some of those individuals in the *Last Verse* of this book. I wish to personally thank the wonderful people of Wyoming and Indiana who have given me the material, background and the personal substance in this endeavor. You were a part of this man's life whether you realized it or not. To the populations of Martinsville, Indiana and those of Gillette, Wyoming; and especially the fine folks of Cheyenne, Wyoming and surrounding areas—you will always maintain a place in my heart. You see...you gave me a home in each of those locations.

I don't know where the trail will go after this book has "gone to market". Like a wilderness path, I search for the rocks stacked carefully along the trail. I enjoy putting my thoughts into written form. Who knows...I could become an "Author" someday. I'd rather tell some more stories instead.

Ron Jordan
Cheyenne, Wyoming
June 29, 2003

Part One: Life in Northern Wyoming

Marks

Use to be that you could look up into the sky at night and gaze at all of the heavenly bodies. On July 20, 1969 that changed when America planted footsteps on the moon's surface, and what was once untouched became just another place we've left a mark upon. "Marks" are what we as Americans are really good at. We "mark" everything, whether it is ours to mark or not. Kind of like "Kilroy was here". We "mark" our vehicles with bumper stickers and decals, our T-shirts with all kinds of advertisement and events, our baseball cap the same. We "mark" our educational institutions with our own version of historical events—what really happened, and the curriculum we teach our kids. We even "mark" our kids according to our own image of what they should become. We "mark" our environment in accordance of what we think the environment should really be like. We "mark" our lives in the belief that in so doing we can understand and associate with ourselves.

I like the freedom a young child has when they color on the walls at home with crayons. My daughter did that before she was even three years old. Of course, Amanda didn't color on the walls to exhibit marking of any kind—she did it because she was excited with the colors and the way they flowed on the white walls. There was no intent of establishing who she was or whose territory it was. She didn't "mark" the walls—she made them beautiful. Of course, at the time as her father, I had to evaluate her own individual expression versus the repair. We say that when our children are that young that they don't know any better. I say, when they're that young they know more than most adults, and it's only through the years that follow that we "mark" them with our do's and don'ts. You can't teach "beauty" or "art" or "individualism" to others. What you have to do is sweep away all of the "marks" in their paths and let them become the person they are destined to become.

1

I can't see the footsteps on the moon's surface from here, but just knowing that someone has left their "mark" there kind of takes some of the beauty out of that lunar wonder. I think that when I leave this world at last, I'd like to do so without leaving a "mark"—just a memory of what was.

Close Call

"Close call!" I've had a few of those in my life time. I've almost drowned, been shot at, been in numerous auto accidents, bucked off horses, to name a few. One that presently sticks in my mind goes back to 1968 when I was a cowboy just north of Cheyenne. It was the typical hot, July day when Rod told Virgil and me to go out to the west range and bring in two range lice eaten bulls so that they could be sprayed. Virgil was a combat vet of World War II who served with the 101st Airborne and who shook hands with General Eisenhower prior to the Normandy Invasion. I was an eighteen year old trying to learn the ropes. Anyway, we left on horseback in the morning and found the two bulls with the rest of the breeding stock several miles west of the ranch proper. Virgil cut out one bull and told me to start heading him back to the ranch corrals while he cut the other bull out of the stock. When I couldn't make the bull head the direction I wanted Virgil said to use a stick or my rope, or run my horse up on the bull's haunch to get him moving. Now range lice can ruin a cattle hide. They also weaken the animal to the extent where they become unresponsive and sluggish. But the bull still weighs 1,500 pounds or more, which makes them pretty darn hard to move. Moving a single bull across the open range requires you to either drive them down a cow path, or along a fence line so that they have some sense of direction of where they're going. While Virgil is back west searching for the other bull, I'm beating myself to death trying to keep this one of mine heading in the right direction. Now, I've driven these bulls as a small herd and crossed the scent of heifers that preceded our paths days in advance. I've seen good bulls just go loco when they picked up the smell of heifers—they go dancing around like 1,500 pound calves. They go through a three strand barbed wire fence like it was kite string. But this bull I was driving seemed pretty docile and sluggish.

Along about a couple of hours later when I was almost back to the corrals, Virgil pulls up on his horse, without the other bull. He couldn't cut him from the herd. Both of us knew then that this was not going to please Rod. Now, these bulls get darn wild out there by themselves. I've seen them take their horns and lift entire sagebrush, roots and all, right out of the ground. Sometimes they fight each other, and either one backs down or the other bull kills it. Long about this time Rod comes tearing out of the corrals on his white roping horse. Our bull recognizes the horse and comes alive. He bolts from Virgil and me and up over the hill he goes.

Now, I wasn't at this time in the good graces with Rod, who then yelled at me, get up there and cut him off! I take off on my cow pony and over the top of the hill I go. The bull is on the other side, panting like he's going to have a cardiac or something. By now I've handed off my rope, and I don't have my stick. But between me and the bull is this small brush pile that just happens to have a proper whacking stick in it. I ride my horse up to the pile, dismount, and while holding my reins with my right hand, bend over to pick up my new stick with my left hand. I see a flash of white beneath my eyes, my horse goes straight up into the air, and I find myself knocked off my feet but still upright. I land on my feet, all the while feeling the reins in my right hand slipping—my horse still dancing on his hind feet, and a sharp pain in my left hip. I now realize that I have just now been charged by the bull, hit, and as I look past me to where the bull is, he is pawing the ground and snorting, ready for the next charge. About that time Virgil appears on top of the hill—yelling to me to get the hell out of there. I yank the reins down sharply, pulling my horse down and spring into the saddle like I had a firecracker up the posterior.

To make this long story shorter—we never got the bull into the corrals, but roped him alongside some planking fence and sprayed him down there. I was so mad afterwards that I stormed back to the bunkhouse, and then examined my left hip. The bull's left horn had been broken from a previous bull fight, so it was snubbed to a blunt eight inches or so. That's what had got me—the blunt side. My hip was black from the bruise I'd received. After that, Rod started calling me "Sir Ronald", took me to Cheyenne Days and paid my way. There might have been some guilt there. He told me later that if the bull hadn't been eaten up with range lice the bull would have killed me right then and there. Said that was a close call! Well, I've had many such close calls since then, but I still remember the day I went dancing with the bull. You can call it luck—I call it fate. I really do believe that when you're number is up, it's up. Close calls are something we all have at times. Funny thing is—I never did hate the bull for what he did. The other part is—the bull is long gone, but I'm still here. Getting ready for my next "close call".

UFO's

I don't think much about it I guess, rather I take it for granted, when I look up into the sky at night and gaze at the billions of stars overhead. A good portion of this country can no longer see the stars of this magnitude either because they live in lighted areas or because of the air pollution. The nearest I can come to the description is, totally black, pierced with white light of such intensity that you can actually see individual stars and the constellations. You crane your head so far back and in all directions in gazing that you become unbalanced. Every now and then you see a particular "star" traveling across the sky—maybe a satellite, but no jet, can climb that high. Sometimes they move in one direction, then change course abruptly, and move off in another direction.

Back in the early 1960's there was a lot of news coverage concerning UFO's. Certain unexplained events took place all over the country. Most folks never saw anything out of the ordinary—most didn't believe the stories anyway. But I recall three particular events on the farm in southern Indiana very vividly. The first was when I was camping out at the end of the farm path with my sisters, Cheri and Kathy. We were still awake and talking in the old green canvas tent—I was lying down on the ground and both of my sisters were in cots on either side of me. The night was clear—not a cloud in the sky and plenty of stars back then. We were jabbering away when all of a sudden the entire tent lit up from an overhead light source so intense that you could read by the light. We froze. After a couple of seconds the light went out, and it was dark again. I got up a few seconds later and went outside the tent and looked into the night sky in all directions. No sound, no wind, no clouds, and no planes—nothing. Just the stars.

A year or so later both of my sisters were playing outside at night on the roof of the old well house. I was inside at the time, when suddenly there were screams and both of them came running into the farm house saying that they had seen a massive black shape with various lights, pass directly over the farm house, without any noise, moving slowly and of very low altitude. I missed that one, and wished I could have seen it. But I did see something else some time later—this time in daylight. I had just closed the corn crib door and was walking down the hill towards the farm house when something caught my eye. It was early evening, the sun had not set in the western horizon yet, and there just above the locust trees was this large metal ball that had the sun bouncing off it like it was made of thousands of mini mirrors. The light was dazzling, bright white and pink hues, all over this ball shape. It moved overhead from my right to left, never wavered with any breeze, and never made a sound. It proceeded on course until it was out of my sight. Nobody else saw it. This observation probably lasted all of thirty seconds or so.

So forty years later, when I gaze up into the heavens, now with my glasses on, I look with wonder at all of those stars. I watch shooting stars, the constellations, and especially those single points of light that move in a direction and with a purpose of their own. And I ask myself—is there something there that I have had contact with in the past? Is it an old friend coming back for another visit, or is it just my own wishful thinking. I enjoy the mystery, and the lack of any definitive answer. Most of all, I am still most grateful for having the privilege of being able to gaze at the stars. And I am humbled by His goodness.

Rocks

Rocks! Jagged rocks, painted rocks, slippery rocks, moss covered rocks, crumbling rocks, pretty rocks, plain rocks, rocks with two legs—I've known a few of those. They're everywhere—rocks. Hard as a rock, dense as a rock, rock-and-roll—I've done that too. I've stumbled over them, climbed them, picked them up, thrown them, and brought them home. I have a pile or rocks just outside the door on the patio. They're stacked-up, just like they are alongside the trail—so you know if you're on the trail or have drifted off course. For me it means, this is where the trail starts, and where it ends. I tell Thomas when we're backpacking and taking a break, and I sit upon a comfortable rock to rest my backpack and my legs, "Ah…This is a GOOD rock!" Never had a pet rock though. Had a lot of pets that were rocks. At any rate—what I'm getting to is this—when you touch a rock, you're touching Mother Earth.

In this world of cement and asphalt, concrete drainage ditches and parking lots—it's hard to connect with the earth. But I bet that there are places in your back yard, at the park, or down the street where, if you wanted, you could find real "earth". In all of our efforts to improve our health—from exercises, to diets, and other forms of healthy living, few address the simple pleasure of connecting with earth. So—try this. Find a good spot on the earth, and sit. Put your arms down to your side, and let your hands touch the earth. Close your eyes, and just relax. I don't want you to meditate or hum, or do yoga or any other funny stuff. Just sit, and feel the earth. Then, I want you to ask yourself when was the last time you sat on the ground?

I figure that for many folks it's been awhile since they connected. As children we did it all the time. Maybe that's why kids are happier than adults. From the earth we came—and to the earth we shall return. That time interval in between, is where we really get messed up. Maybe that's why there are so many rocks.

Stage Coach

The wood creaked and groaned when I stepped aboard. The springs that bolted the carriage to the axle shifted in a wayward motion from side to side when I took my place onboard the coach. I pulled the door closed and rolled the curtain down to keep the scorching sun from beating directly on me. It was hot, and I was sweating beneath the woolen shirt and canvas trousers I had on. I leaned back in the wooden bench and tried to find a comfortable position for the long ride on the trail ahead.

I had purchased my ticket just an hour before, lucky that I was able to get passage on this coach leaving out of Cheyenne and heading to Deadwood. It was early August, and an unseasonably dry year. I glanced at the other passengers, said my hellos, and looked out between the curtain and the window as the coach bolted forward. Immediately there was fine dust in the air and the floorboard rocked from side to side and backward to forward again. I could hear the crack of a whip as the teamster shouted out to the team, and the stage gained speed. Well over a hundred miles to go, but I considered myself fortunate not to have attempted this trip on the highway alone. I had business to take care of in Deadwood and if time permitted, I might even get in a few rounds of poker.

I shifted my holster more to my side so the .44 would not gouge me as we rolled north out of Cheyenne and crested the first hill along the trail. The dust was choking, the heat unbearable, and the constant motion of the stage kept me from finding any real comfortable position. This highway we were traveling was much better that it had been previously and I counted my blessings. At least I wasn't traveling some interstate in the year 2000, looking for rest areas, filling stations and a place to eat every fifty miles. Or listening to some whining kid in the back seat complaining they didn't have anything to do or that they were bored. That, and having to put up with air conditioning and tinted windows that didn't allow you to feel the journey you were undertaking. And I wouldn't have to worry about somebody falling asleep at the wheel resulting in a head on collision just because they were too lazy to get out from behind the wheel and take a break. No other any stages were tailgating us today either. And we don't have to worry about going too fast because we have to make the horses last to the next station where we can switch them out. No road construction to hinder us, no billboards or signs to blight the landscape. No cell phone to make you feel safe—that's what the .44 is for. No sir, this trip like any other trip requires just a little planning and foresight. Not one of those—jump in your auto and hope you get there alive.

I reached into my breast pocket and pulled out my flask. I offered the other three passengers a drink then had one myself. Cuts the dust and puts a better light on things I think. We'd be together for awhile on this trip so we might as well enjoy each other's company. No road rage out here. I settled back in my seat, appreciative that the late 1800's were still here. If I were alive in another hundred years I sure would pity those poor travelers then. The teamster yells down to us that it's only about another twenty miles or so to the first station and supper will be waiting. Says that the gal there can really rustle up a good spread. Sounds good to me, as I roll up the window curtain and look out upon the evening landscape. It's much cooler now and the sun is sinking in the west. This is the makings of a good journey, and I should make more of them.

Simpler Life

I remember a time when life was simpler. It was a long time ago. When I was a boy I recall reading about a Civil War Veteran still alive and who was a drummer boy during the Civil War. I remember a time without illegal drugs. There had been no one on the moon yet, or even in space. There were no computers, or even calculators. On the farm your phone was part of a "party line". There were two other families that shared the same line as we did. There were no microwaves, or colored television. The black and white "tube" was on only certain times of the day. No FM radio. Country music was "country". Airplanes were just that—not jets. The eight track wasn't even around yet. Still had records—78's, 33's and the new 45's. There were three sports in school—baseball, football and basketball. Cigarettes didn't even have filters then. You could still roll your own. Bull Durham was the best tobacco. You didn't have to lock your house up when you went to town. You could leave your keys in the ignition at night and everything would be where you left it, in the morning. Driving a farm tractor down a country road to another field was an experience and certain freedom. The smell of new mown hay and the crickets at night.

I remember picking wild blackberries and raspberries and eating more than I took home. I remember working the garden—from planting to harvest. I could go down the farm path with a salt shaker in my hand and pick a tomato for a snack. Drinking a Pepsi or Coke was a treat. A bottle cost a nickel. A pack of five slices of gum cost a penny. A candy bar was five cents and larger than today's candy bar. I remember gathering empty bottles along the roadside and taking them in to the grocery for deposit. I remember my first school dance and how awkward I felt.

I remember my first school sweetheart and how pretty she was. I remember camping out under the stars at ten years of age by myself without real fear—except for all of the night noises. So many noises, but all comforting somehow. I remember my first dog and how I loved her. I remember the long hikes we took together through the countryside. I remember my first rifle my Dad gave me for Christmas when I was ten. I could buy .22 shells at Sears or Montgomery Wards and target shoot all day. We didn't have Wal Mart or K Mart back then. I remember when there were no malls, just downtown stores. People knew who you were by name.

There was respect for others and their property then. Somehow giving respect earned you respect from others. Your elders, your parents, grandparents and teachers. I remember the dreams of youth—and how you could be anything you wanted to be when you grew up. The world was big, but personal. Maybe some day I'll write a book about the times when life was simpler. Times may have changed, but the memories, ah the memories—they linger still.

Education

My mind went blank and my pulse quickened. I felt a certain cold dampness on my forehead as the world started to spin. I knew I had the answer tucked away somewhere in the back of my head, but I just couldn't locate it. What was even worse was the fact that I was now being scrutinized by all those eyes upon me. Did those folks know the answer, or were they just glaring at me to see if I would crumble? Why didn't I go over my notes more thoroughly, and in particular, this area I was being questioned about?

It was a time like this that I felt the whole academia world was making a fool of me. I could make a fool of myself without any of their assistance, thank you! I started to speak, but hesitated. No need to rush on this response, regardless of the number of folks staring at me. The plain fact of the matter was this—I just didn't have an answer. Well, I did have an answer…but not the one the teacher was looking for. So, I threw out the only response I had at the time…"Ma'am, I just don't know". And I sat back down in my seat. The pressure was off, and she was looking for new prey. Years later, when I look back at those tough times in school and the classes I took, and the various pressures I grew to accept as I inched my way through elementary, secondary, high school and later the university, I realize now that those "pressures" were actually self-inflicted.

I have come to understand that no one person can know all of the answers. And I have also come to respect those individuals who consistently strive to improve their minds through continuing education. Even more importantly, I now realize that's it not how much of an education one has but rather, how they incorporate it in their lives. If anything, an education should teach one to "learn" to find the answers, not provide the actual answers. And, I think I have learned something else. In measuring a person's knowledge it would be wise to first evaluate the "yardstick" we wield in that measurement. Standards of measurement are not "standard".

No Water

Yesterday and today it was in the high 90's—like maybe the 100's. Yesterday afternoon a water main broke that was a main line for the community where we live. So I called them up. "What's the status of our water?" I ask. "Well, they should have it back on around 8:00 to 8:30 p.m.", was the reply. "If it's not back on by then—call us back." So I'm thinking to myself—duh, they think I'm going to call them back to let them know that that I still don't have water, right!

Thomas came home last night from work—no water. He went back to the church youth building and took a shower. I gave him four 5-gallon water jugs to fill-up just in case. Good assumption on my part because by 10:00 p.m. last night still no water. This morning—still no water. I drove around the community last night but found nobody working on anything, anywhere. When I got home from work this evening, we had water again. So if you want to "feel" how a raging lunatic feels, turn your own water off for a couple of days. We use it for our swamp cooler (no air conditioning), morning coffee, showers, and laundry, toilets, drinking (that's an important one there), washing dishes, watering the plants; it keeps the cats and dog alive too. Oh sure, I can take twenty gallons out with me and Thomas to the scorching Grasslands and make it last three days. Don't need much to wash yourself down, brush your teeth, wash your hands, cook and give to Tippy. Roughing it! But when I'm back in "civilization" I expect the same facilities the rest of the town has at the time. It was Sunday when we lost the water supply. Government utility employees don't work on Sundays—why should they when they don't work the rest of the week either! Water is a very precious resource. When I figure family usage for my customers I use a simple formula. Basically, it's 75 gallons a day, per person in the household. Now, most folks can figure that out for a family of four to be around 2,100 gallons a week for the household. But since government utility employees are not paid to think, and they have they're own water at home, the fact that you have zero gallons on hand is something they are not concerned about. And the fact that you pay your water bill based upon usage doesn't matter either. "Hey—I got my paycheck, and it's the weekend!"

Now I don't want to sound like a grumbling customer. I don't want to sound as if I can't put up with a little inconvenience, even if it's normally no water at times, at least once a month. And I don't want to think I'm a belligerent, so-and-so. No Sir! I want to make sure that I'm fair and set the example as an upstanding citizen of my community. That's why, if when I got home from work today and still found we had no water, I was going to be fair, and make each bullet count for every bureaucrat that I found going home at five o'clock. Seriously though, (I thought I was serious) it irks me to know that apathy rules the day. It's a good thing I wasn't around for our Civil War. I would have fought for the South, and Robert E. Lee, and my home. And I would have died doing it. Because the alternative—well the alternative is, what we have today.

The Military

"I, _____, do solemnly swear (or affirm) that I will support and defend the Constitution of the United States against all enemies, foreign and domestic; that I will bear true faith and allegiance to the same; and that I will obey the orders of the President of the United States and the orders of the officers appointed over me, according to regulations and the Uniform Code of Military Justice. So help me God." That's the Oath of Enlistment you take when you're willing to sign-up, or re-enlist. It doesn't mean squat to Joe Public. He's cool—he just doesn't want to be in the Military.

He's not as cool as he thinks though. In this age of declining morals and doing anything worthwhile, Joe Public comes in dead last. You see, when I was in the Army Recruiting Command I knew what it took to enlist—and the majority of Americans didn't qualify, including Joe Public. Why? Three primary reasons. The first was health. Over half of the American public is overweight and not qualified (body fat included). That and all of their health problems with other things like broken bones with pins, asthma, high blood pressure, allergies etc. Second problem. Over half of the public could not get a fifty or above on the Armed Services Vocational Aptitude Battery (ASVAB) test. Doesn't mean that they were totally stupid—just meant that they weren't smart enough. And third, there was the problem with law violations. In other words, they weren't the "upstanding" citizen they thought they were. Outstanding fines, court appearances still pending, serious law violations in the past, felonies, to name a few.

So that left me with about ten percent of the public "pool" to recruit from. Of course, you had to find someone that, even though they qualified, still wanted to join up. The Oath of Enlistment our Service Member takes not only affects them personally, but the lives and welfare of the husbands, wives, sons and daughters of their immediate family. It boils down to "Sacrifice", for each and every one of them. And yet this great Nation of ours continues to undermine their existence, and that of their families. Each year there are fewer and fewer benefits for those on active duty. Even fewer for the Veterans that proudly served their Nation. Each Service Member, and their Family Member, is a True Patriot. They do on a daily basis what the majority of the public refuses to do throughout their lives. They put their lives on the line daily, and the lives of their Family Members on hold, just so they can honorably serve Joe Public. Look at how many of our elected officials have any military background—especially in Congress. Make that comparison today with what it was when this Nation of ours was given its birth by our Forefathers. Is it any wonder that the Service Member and their Families today bears the brunt of a non-caring public and our elected officials?

If you're one of the Joe Public, and think that you're cool, and that you didn't join the Military because you were too good for that sort of thing—well, I just want to enlighten you a tad. You're living a lie. My heart and my respect still goes to those who unselfishly serve this Nation of ours in uniform, and their Families. God have mercy on the non-caring public and their elected officials!

Fires

The smoke hangs in the air here tonight. The type of smoke that smells like a campfire—only it's not a campfire burning, but the prairie. It's even inside the house presently, sucked in by the swamp cooler. These last couple of weeks have seen a number of uncontrolled burns throughout Wyoming, Colorado and Montana. Couple of days ago we got the smoke from Montana—tonight it is more local. Two weeks ago when Thomas and I were returning from South Dakota and we were about twenty miles just east of Gillette on Interstate 90, we watched as the lightening set five different fires to the prairie on both sides of the Interstate. The wind was so strong that I thought a couple of times the sheer effect would lift the jeep right off the Interstate. We watched the orange flames lick at the grasses, as the black and white smoke rose into the air.

Fire, in Nature, has a cleansing effect. Burns out the sage and dry grasses, and makes a home for new growth. When the sun sets in the horizon at night it is an orange ball in a haze. This morning we actually had dew on everything—but it was soon in the 90's and the heat returned. I've walked through many burned-out areas, both in the forests and the prairie. The prairie recovers more quickly, the forest takes generations. For man, he nearly always chooses to intervene in fires. Sometimes in Nature that is good—most of the time it's not. It just prolongs the impending disaster that will eventually overcome Man's ability to combat the fire.

We tend to think that we can control our environment, or "manage" it as we say. And we can, for awhile. But it is Nature's way to let us know up front on many occasions that no matter how confident we feel in our ability to regulate the outcome, she will put us on our knees and humble us as nobody else possibly can. There's a certain beauty in that, if not comfort. For no matter how badly we screw things up for ourselves in this world, Nature will still take her course. So, as I sit here typing another "Considerations" this evening, and breathe the smoke of life that has entered my realm, I am reminded that for all of our endeavors, we're really still "runts" when it comes to a true understanding of where we fit in this world of ours. The gray skies, smoke-filled air, and orange sunsets are just little reminders that our hold on this Planet of ours is at best, precarious.

Cowboy Hats

Hot and dry—wind takes the moisture right out of you. Temperature in the 100's, no rain, orange sunsets and hazy mornings. Sweat running down the sides of one's face and across the forehead. August days on the High Plains in Wyoming. Levis and cow-kicking boots. In town it's a baseball cap—out of town in the wide open places, wool felt cowboy hat with a wide brim. No real cowboy would wear a straw hat—though one sees them on a lot of folks who might look like a cowboy. I tried a straw cowboy hat, once. Sure, it's lighter in weight, and would appear to keep your head cooler, but it isn't "cowboy". It won't shed rain, won't keep still in the wind (it's like tying a kite to your head and having your neck jerk one way then another), won't stay on your head in the breeze, won't keep your head warm in the Winter, won't regain it's shape once you mash it, roll on it, or sit on it. It's "Hollywood" though, so that basically means it's worthless. It'd work back east in the high humidity, no wind, city-slicker ways. When I see a straw hat on a fellow out here I think to myself—nice try.

I know—I'm being critical about preferences here. The other thing is the styles of all of the hats, straw and felt—there isn't any of those either. They're all the same "rancher style". The first thing I did with my hat when I got it was to break it in—I tore out the liner inside, filled it with water, and reshaped it to my own individual style. The only thing it hasn't seen yet is cow manure. I do have some pride.

I was looking and trying on some new hats in a couple of the western outfitting stores here and in South Dakota several weeks ago. I was interested in the Stetsons of course—$150.00 or up, not out of the price range either. You get what you pay for. If you want to look like Little Abner in a rainstorm by a cheap hat. If you want to look like a drenched cowboy in a rainstorm, buy a good hat. Anyway, I couldn't find a Stetson I liked, or that fit as good as the hat I still wear—so no buy. I looked in my catalogs and on the internet and was amazed when they all stated that it was not recommended that their hats be worn in the rain! I'm still trying to figure that out—must be the style changes in the rain and you're not an Aristocrat anymore. I could have settled for another brand—but who wants to look like a Polyester Pilgrim! I'll stick to my boots, Levis and felt hat.

When it comes to dressing up I can always put on an ironed long-sleeve shirt, my vest, clean jeans, polish my boots, strap on a good belt buckle, and brush my felt hat. It's not "Designer", but it makes for a better statement about practicality. And as long as I stay in these parts, nobody looks at me twice.

Tippy

A man's love! She was so young when I stopped by ten years ago. She was with her mother and another of her siblings. I don't know what attracted me to her; perhaps it was the brown eyes. Or the way she tilted her head and looked at me. She was excited beyond reason at my approach. You could see that it flowed through her, and I fell in love. I touched her head—she licked my face and jumped with joy. I filled out the forms at the animal shelter and became the adopted master of a six week old puppy. They told me then that this puppy, the rest of the litter, and its mother were scheduled to be put asleep in the morning. I took her with me to her new home.

The first night outside she whimpered all night. I fixed a special area for her in the garage that she could call her own. Next morning she followed me everywhere I went. I played with her, ran with her, tossed the ball, and acquired a number of chew toys for her. She was always under foot—never wanting to let me out of sight. She whimpered yesterday when I left her behind as I ventured out onto the prairie alone. In the past she has scouted for me, let me know when something was there in the dark that I couldn't see or hear, and has forgiven me for every harsh rebuke and punishment that I dealt her.

She is courageous beyond her size. Her heart is even bigger. She has rolled in some of the most pungent perfumes and willingly shared them with me with happiness. She has eaten things that surpass road-kill. She has waded in the foulest of mud holes and chased birds until I thought she would take flight herself. She has missed the sight and smell of small wildlife within feet of her, and lost track of other animals when they have taken a sudden turn within her vision. Cold evenings she will rest her head on my feet as I sit in the chair. I bring her inside at nights when I go to bed and she lays inside the closed bedroom door so that no one can enter the bedroom without first moving her. She will do the same thing at my campsite—sleeping in front of the tent flap outside at night. She can catch a tennis ball thrown twenty feet into the air and bring it back to me for another throw. Around two o'clock in the morning I take her outside and give her milk bone biscuits and her water for breakfast, then padlock the gate. She goes back to sleep and so do I.

When I come home from work she is always excited to see me—or anytime I return from being gone, even a short time. I can rub behind her ears, or hold a front paw and massage her leg while she closes her eyes and sighs. No stranger can approach me without her going on the attack. Every dog in the neighborhood can be barking around her, yet she remains quiet unless she herself is threatened, or they enter the yard or look suspicious. She doesn't like the Schwann truck, UPS, or police cars that drive to slow in the neighborhood. She allows our cats to bat, hiss, and be down right mean to her, and ignores them. She gets even when her tail slaps them in the face accidentally. I make the one special sound I have for her and she comes to me immediately. "Tippy". A name that doesn't sound too original—but she is.

And I would protect, care and nourish her beyond any reason and any cost. True loyalty has no price. Ten years ago those wonderful brown eyes, wagging tail and wriggling body that went every direction at once, captured my heart. I am filled with sorrow when I cannot do enough for her, like take her with me whenever I go on one of my journeys. She's an older dog now—but how much we have both shared in our experiences together. Tippy has enriched my life and brought into focus what a true relationship is all about.

Man's best friend? That and more...

Wild Horses

Rod brought in a small herd of horses that hadn't seen the sight of man for a couple of years. His intent was to rid himself of grass burners that hadn't been of any benefit to the ranch for some time. His plan…was for me to "tame" these critters to the extent where he could ride them around in the auction arena and get a decent price for them. These horses spoke danger. Tails that reached to the ground and manes that flowed to their shoulders, eyes white with fear and trepidation. They didn't enjoy the company of man. So I worked them, trying to tame their fears and wildness. I would choose one and work with that particular horse until I felt that at least it showed some semblance of civility.

One late afternoon, Rod told me to go out and bring in the two Brown Swiss milk cows—take a wild one to herd them back to the corals. "Okay", I replied and went to the corral and picked one I thought I could handle. Macho me, no saddle—just go out and get those cows. Off I went, literally. Several times, actually. I finally was able to maintain some authority over the beast when I would find myself on the ground again. An hour went by, then another hour. Between trying to maintain my "seat" and looking for the milk cows out on the range, somewhere, I was getting nowhere.

I returned to the corrals leading my horse and nursing my backside. Rod met me—"Where have you been?" "Looking for the damn cows", I replied. He told me that Virgil had already gotten them in the barn and was almost done milking them. "What are you walking that horse for?" he asked. I told him that I had been every which way from sundown on this particular animal and was tired of eating the dirt. He told me to give the horse to him and he'd show me how to work him. He swung up on the horse's back and proceeded to ride him rough style along the planking fence inside the corral—first one direction, then another. Cutting him hard one way, then another. "See…You got to get control of him—let him know you mean business!" he said. He rode the horse hard, turned him sharply and went airborne into the fence planking, crashing into the dirt. "I see what you mean…Rod. I think I've been there myself." Rod dusted himself off and replied, "Well that's enough for one day!"

Later, he took that small herd to the auction arena, but didn't ride any of them—leaving the question of "tameness" for the bidders to interpret for themselves. Anyway, we were rid of them. Somehow, my pride wasn't bruised. As a matter of fact—it was boosted. Just knowing that the ranch foreman couldn't keep his seat either did wonders for my ego. They say that "Misery loves company". I'd say that we were just "sharing experiences".

The Ledge

Weightlessness. Stand on the edge and look down, and let the distance below rush up at you as if you had fallen. Stay too long on the ledge and you lose you're sense of balance. You strain your eyesight to depict the minutest details so far beneath your feet. You've never been where you're looking. Perhaps nobody has been there—it's inaccessible. The wind roars into your face, which is okay. It's the gusts from behind that causes concern. With your feet just inches away from the drop-off, and the gusts from behind you, you start to wonder just what it would take to physically blow you over the ledge. A forty mph wind gust? Sixty mph? Could you recover in time before you found yourself falling? And always there is that thought that once you depart this ledge there is no turning back—no second chance. It's thousands of feet to the bottom. You see where great slabs of rock have been sliced off of the rock face and where they have plowed a huge furrow in the glacier below.

This is Nature at work—the glaciers, the deep green lakes, the cold wind that chaps and burns the face, eyes watering, shivering from the cold wind. How close you are in joining the forces of nature—of becoming "one" with all before your view. Perhaps that is why, when we desire and must have our solitude, and time for peaceful reflection, a chance to collect our thoughts and further evaluate who we are and where we should fit into this world of ours—that we seek the comfort of Nature.

Sometimes it is better not to think, or to contemplate about those things that cause us concern. Perhaps, just to take the time for reflection, without arriving at any conclusion. No answers—no solutions, just drifting. Sometimes, just placing your entire life at the mercy of the environment, or standing on the ledge—is enough to give you a better understanding and interpretation of life.

Older

Sometimes I feel older. Today it rained—first in a long time, and a cold front has now blown in. Suppose to get down in the 40's tonight and only in the 70's tomorrow. Today Thomas started his first day of school for the year—a senior in High School. Tomorrow Amanda turns twenty-two years of age. Thomas and I are leaving this Saturday for Denver to visit her for the weekend and to celebrate her birthday. Maybe it's the season—or maybe it's just that fall has arrived earlier than usual with school, a birthday and colder weather. But I do feel older. Certainly no wiser though.

Fall is a time for reflection. It has something to do with a summer that's over and days that are shorter. I really don't need the darkness to come any earlier—I have enough trouble seeing things in the light. Perhaps the One above does this to me just to see if I can handle the change or not. Oh, I know—I've seen fifty different years of seasonal changes and that in itself should reconcile one to make the necessary adjustments that are on the horizon. But somehow the different changes around me make me feel older. No matter how many times you experience the same changes they always seem different. Unique in their own way.

When I think about it though—nothing ever stays the same. There are "seasons" wherever you go in the world, regardless of the environment or however miniscule they may seem. I guess that's what makes life interesting—just when you think you've got a handle on things; it changes into a different picture with hues, colors, and tones you haven't quite experienced before. If that's "growing pains" then maybe I'm not getting older after all. Could it be that I have finally discovered "eternal youth"? Naw—I still feel older…

Wood Rots

Wood rots, rocks crumble and vegetation dies. We spend most of our lives building, remodeling, painting, and tending to our vegetation. We build something new, and in later years make repairs by sections. New wood against weathered boards, new paint over aged paint, fresh mortar patched in cracks. Steel posts mixed in with wood fence posts. Rusted barbed wire tied to new wire. Plumbing fixtures replaced. Dead trees cut for firewood and young trees nourished for growth and shade. Gardens and fields planted then harvested. The process continues throughout our lives. A Blossom turns into an apple, a pod into a bean.

I have always been fascinated by the past and trying to interpret what was. On the old farmstead in southern Indiana back by the old barn on the hill there is a small depression in the ground. It lies just east of the barn alongside a ravine and just south of a small hill. There one will find several large rocks positioned on the lip of this small depression. Look closely and one can imagine the outline of some past building that stood at this spot—the rocks being the cornerstones of its foundation. In days long gone, large rocks were used as the foundation that supported the upright beams for the corner walls of buildings and kept the lumber from rotting. This process was used for barns and houses alike. Before days of abundant concrete and steel. What structure stood there? The lumber used was what we called "native wood"—cut while still green and later hardened to the point where it was next to impossible to drive a nail into it in later years. Walls were constructed using the same wood as "slats" with mortar inserted between the slats, much like the old cabin construction. Same with the ceilings. Doors were constructed of solid planks. Interior doors even had overhead openings much like windows that allowed air to circulate within the various rooms to provide warmth in the winter. Central heating was just that—central. Rooms furthest away from the heat source were the coldest in winter. Light was provided by coal fuel lamps—adjusted by turning the wick up or down. Canned goods from that year's garden were kept in a cellar, which was dug out under the home and lined with stone. Wood planking shelves sat upon a dirt floor and contained all of the various canned goods in Ball jars for that year's harvest.

Home luxuries might include a roofed porch—where one could sit and watch the sunsets, or listen to the patter of the rain on a cloudy day and feel the breeze at night. Lightening rods could be found on the highest points of roofs for homes and barns, with grounding cables running to and anchored into the ground. In later years when electricity was an added feature one could find electrical wires attached to porcelain spool insulators in the attic. Electricity arrived by wire attached to blue glass insulators atop poles along the road. Indoor plumbing consisted of a well pump in the "kitchen" which required the effort of pumping the handle. A long rod ran the length inside of a steel pipe on the end of which consisted a series of leather plungers or washers which when wet, provided the suction or vacuum to draw the water up through the pipe by the pumping action above.

One took baths with water heated over a stove. In the summer one could pleasantly scrub down outside. Most windows and doors faced to the south—away from the harsh winds, but allowing for warmth from the sun low in the winter skies. Windows opened straight up in the summer, while the glass frosted and was cold to the touch in the winter months. "Paths" were formed in the yard instead of sidewalks. Of particular importance was a shoveled path through the snow to the old outhouse. The luxuries of outhouse accommodations included a small coal fuel heater for the cold and a coal oil lamp for the darkness. Of course there were always all those little critters that usually moved into the outhouse to keep one company—spiders and snakes included. Visits were kept short and "primping before a mirror" unheard of. Pure basics. After a few years the outhouse was moved over to another new hole and the old hole covered up. Lime took care of all the required sanitation.

Barns always had a loft to store hay in. In days before bailing, hay was put up loose. A track ran the interior peak of the barn roof and utilized a lift system incorporating large hooks for lifting the hay to the loft. A covered overhang allowed the hooks to descend outside the barn while pulling ropes ran through the interior and out a back barn opening. This allowed use of a pulley system to lift the hay up through the covered overhang and then roll on the rail inside where a trip rope would open the hooks and allow the hay to fall into position in the loft. It was pitched-forked into just the right places. Hay was fed out to the cattle and horses in the winter and provided plenty of hiding places for the chickens to lay eggs in which to gather, or to find new-borne chicks. One reached the loft by climbing a ladder straight up. Getting the eggs down without breaking them was a separate problem.

I lived portions of this life I have described in earlier days—fitting in somewhere between the past and what was then the present. Wood rots, rocks crumble and vegetation dies. What once was—is now a slight depression in the ground. Memories fade with the person's departure. And still I wonder…

Denver Trip

Different worlds. That's what it feels like when this boy from the country visits a place like Denver. Take for example, traffic and fast-moving life styles. Events going on all the time. Want to watch the most recent movie at the local theater? You have twenty-four theaters in one building to choose from. Want to eat? Get there early and bring your wallet. Want to go somewhere? Tighten your seatbelt and pray that your vehicle has the capability to go from zero to hell in ten seconds, and that your brakes don't fail at the next stop light. (I'll need to install afterburners on the Jeep for the next visit.)

This old boy has a heck of a time trying to prevent whip lash just from watching all of the drivers maneuver about me. To keep up with the traffic flow one has to bury his accelerator into the floorboard with one foot and crystallize his disc brakes with the other foot. I know that I get the benefit of doubt driving around in a vehicle with Wyoming license plates, windows down and wearing my cowboy hat. People don't get too close to you. They know you're not of their world.

I don't get uncomfortable much if I keep my anxiety attacks under control. When my daughter drives me around in Denver I keep pumping the brake pedal on the passenger side—but to no avail. She enjoys the fast-pace, lots of stuff to do, ever-changing world she lives in—but doesn't enjoy the traffic either. But she's more adaptable than I'll ever be, so she can cope with the "flow". I get lost on the streets trying to find my way around. The only way I can make it back to her place is to have the mountains and the sun in view so I know where I am.

Street names mean nothing to me. Besides, I can't read them anyway when I'm doing sixty in a thirty mph zone, and I'm holding up the traffic.

I enjoy visiting a place like Denver for a number or reasons. Most importantly my daughter lives there and is the most gracious host a father could ask for. She understands me. I also enjoy watching all of the different kinds of folks there. All kinds of ethnic origins, shapes, sizes and expressions. Every now and then I run across someone who has that glazed look in the eyes like myself and I'm not sure if they're lost like me of if they're on drugs. I'm not a womanizer—but there are some beautiful women in Denver. (Louisville still has the best fillies of anywhere though.) Money—boy is there money in a place like Denver! Nothing is cheap. We went to a new mall that my daughter wanted to show me. We looked around some and I decided to get some espresso coffee because my stress level was getting low. This gal gives me a quarter-filled mini bathroom cup of espresso coffee and told me that it was $1.45, plus twelve percent tax. I always try to be nice to any waitress, clerk or salesperson I deal with because they have the worst of any situation with customers. That's the only thing that kept me from jumping over the counter and wrecking the place. I was nice though. I took my mini cup and slugged it down. Then we went over to Starbuck's and I got a big cup of coffee for a buck-thirty. I wanted to get a new Stetson so we went over to another shopping center where I found just the hat. I told the guy (who was moving back to Cody, Wyoming) that he would have a real happy customer if he could knock-off $1.45 on the hat—that way I'd at least break even. He knocked off five bucks instead. The hat still cost me $135.00 but I got a bargain in the deal.

I found that if I wanted to get around "town" on my own that all I had to do was drive the streets at six o'clock in the morning. The sun's up, the air is clear, and the bumper car derby is a couple of hours away yet. My son and I had a wonderful time during our visit. We departed Denver and headed 325 miles to the north. After one gets past Cheyenne things really slow down. The landscape begins to roll out on all sides. Traffic consists of a occasional truck and horse trailer or a wandering RV'er. When we got north of Douglas, Wyoming there were more vehicles with Colorado plates going south than what there were drivers going north. Guess they got a taste of the Frontier over the weekend. They were heading back to their world and we were heading towards ours. Made me think though—which direction "civilization" was located?

Winter

This weekend was spent preparing for Old Man Winter. Under the house checking insulation and heat cord around the water lines, plugging in the heat cords and testing for operation, painting last minute things outside, cutting the grass and trimming—and wondering if this would be the last time for that. Still have storm windows to reinstall but the days can still become warm in September. Still have some roof work to look at before the cold weather arrives. Looking at the wood pile to be sure there's enough wood for the stove in case the power goes for a couple of days. While the summer months in Wyoming can become unbearable with the temperatures reaching into the hundreds, winter can just flat out kill you.

There have been folks caught out in the open without proper clothing and shelter that never came home. I think that we're going to have a tough winter here this year—maybe the whole country. The "signs" are there for a sudden arrival that could plunge this country into a winter-chill that won't let up until spring. We're overdue for sure. Reminds me of all those things that must be done—or suffer the consequences for neglect. I always think that I've prepared properly for the cold, but I still check and recheck.

I lighted the furnace a couple of nights ago and have had the heat on a couple of times already at night. I wonder about some folks whose everyday life is "summer" until the car won't start or gets stuck with lousy tires. Or their water lines freeze and burst. Or the furnace quits on them. They say that the wind-chill has no effect on inanimate objects such as machinery etc. I know that isn't true because I've personally stood still in a winter breeze until I became "inanimate" and I still felt the cold. The cold brings out the best and worst in folks. The "best" are individuals helping others in their desperate time of need. The "worst" are the things that happen every winter—such as heating oil shortages and higher gouging prices. Electric bills that climb in cost.

But for a guy like myself I'm sometimes more concerned with staying upright when I walk out the door on a winter morning. I can locate a patch of ice without even looking for it. I've done more "doughnuts" with my vehicles in a single day that would put a baker's dozen to shame. I've gone places unintentionally in my vehicles that I didn't even know they were capable of doing—and lived to tell about it. It's the other guy I worry about. Those with the rear-wheel drive clunker and bald tires negotiating an icy corner doing thirty miles an hour. Even then, I start sweating at twenty below zero. We get so accustomed to driving during the summer months that we have to learn all over again when the cold weather arrives. Like our learning curve is nonexistent. For those of us without garages, each morning begins with trying to get the vehicle started and the windows warmed up enough so one doesn't have to use a chisel and hammer to get the ice off the glass. I've broken more ice scrapers in my hand than I can remember—usually when I'm in a rush to get somewhere. I try to remember to wear my gloves so that I don't bleed all over the place when the ice scraper snaps in my hand.

Oh yea—ever notice how your skin turns into cracked lizard leather? I have to use super glue to keep the cuts closed so that they will heal. What little hair that I have on my head goes straight to dandruff—I look like I've been out in the snow all winter long. I've always wondered how the wind can blow up your coat. It doesn't blow up your shirts in summer—at least I don't feel it. I can remember it being so cold at times that the snot freezes inside your nose. How's that for bringing back those romantic memories? I've barely jammed my fingers in the cold but would swear that someone just used a sledgehammer on them.

Many times I've lain out on the ice looking up at the sky and wondered just how I got there. I didn't remember falling down—I can even get on the ground that fast if I tried. Yes—fall is moving right along and winter is not far behind. I'll have to readjust my life style again to just plain survival. It's odd how we take things for granted—first we're a grasshopper, then we're wishing we were an ant. By the time spring comes around again we're all Polar Bears.

Little People

Kids! I enjoy the little people. There's a certain innocence that little kids have about them—even when they have done something wrong. I'm talking about kids that are two years old to say, eight years old. You can't blame them for doing something wrong—for two primary reasons. One reason is they don't know any better—kind of like the Private in the Army. The second reason is that their parents (every kid has two, whether they're together or not) most likely don't know what their kids are doing at the time of their wrongdoing.

I met a little boy today on one of my service calls who had only two miniature teeth at the bottom gum line—and he wanted to talk. So did I—but I listened to him instead. (I've found out that when I let the little people talk that I learn more than I would by talking myself.) Little girls and boys don't have prejudices, animosities or attitudes—unless the adults have been working on them. So anything they tell me is the truth. Now when you stop and think about it—when was the last time you had a conversation with a stranger that you didn't have to try and second-guess any possible "motives" they might have had for your hearing interpretation? Little people are a lot smarter than I am. They see things in a uncorrupted light that makes you think of changing your own perspectives about things. Little people don't have to think when they ask "Why?"—They just want to know. Of course we have to think about how to answer the question…"Why?" We usually answer with something that is a plausible explanation or reason. Little people don't care about plausible explanations or reasons—they just want to know…"Why?" Now if you don't believe that just answer the question incorrectly and I'll bet you get another question of…"Why?" See—little people keep us on our toes. What we think is a plausible and rational explanation doesn't mean squat in their interpretation of things. And we thought we were so smart!

Anyway, this little boy on the service call that I made today bade me farewell when I was done at his home. He did this by pointing to his bottom gum line and announced "Teeth!" I was in no position to dispute his statement because he was absolutely correct. See—one word said a book about the description and feelings of his new teeth. I've known people who could talk all day and not say anything substantial. (Hum…maybe I better quit now.)

Divorce

As I write these "Considerations" I attempt to place emphasis on things that I feel should be of some importance to others in the way of humor, anecdotes, perspectives and at times, things of personal nature that I have encountered—in the hope of widening the "horizons" of others. I don't think that I am always successful in all areas at all times. So this time around I'll share with you the subject of "sadness". Now, sadness comes in many shapes and forms. We all have encountered our share, to be sure. So when Karla came home today from her last store in Utah and announced that she was filing for divorce you can be assured that I encountered my share of sadness for one day. All I could think about were the twenty-four years together, the times shared good and bad, and all the things I could have done better.

Karla's Mother is dying from cancer and her life expectancy is less than a year. That too is sadness. Karla has decided to finish up with her last store in Cheyenne beginning Friday, and then will move back to Columbia City, Indiana to be with her Mother. Wyoming will no longer be her home. That is also sadness.

People change throughout their lives—and sometimes those changes become so different that the person you once knew is no longer the same person. "Distance" becomes more prevalent with time, until the space is so vast that nothing can cross it. I had the thought of trying to work something out. But Karla's mind is made up. I am a fighter by nature. I don't enjoy going into battle, fighting anything and everything that crosses my path. One has to be selective I guess, and so I gave thought of fighting this event as well. But you don't fight the ones you love. In the Army I learned to fold and case the Regimental Colors when the unit was deactivated. Perhaps that is what this is—deactivation of a marriage. I like the term "deactivation" better than "divorce". Casing the Colors was sadness as well. The last Hurrah!

I don't know what life has in store for me—nor does anyone for that matter. I've learned that "Character" has nothing to do with who you are, but rather "what" you are made of. There are some things in my nature that I know folks could find fault with. I'm far from perfect. But certain things I cannot let go. My daughter and son are the most precious people in my life. Amanda lives in Denver and Thomas will remain living with me through his last year in high school—each has their own life to live and I respect their wishes. Karla will move back to Indiana because she wants to, and I'll respect her wishes too. I will remain in Wyoming. There too, is sadness.

Sometimes "Distance" is borne out of love as well. Throughout my life I've have been in some very difficult situations. This is one of those times. I do believe in the old adage that what doesn't kill you makes you stronger. I have no hatred, contempt or bitterness—just sadness. I want no pity, no sympathy or empathy. There are a lot of feelings in tears…a lot of sadness. But both should become the new foundation of strength and stability. And so I share this with you—count your blessings, each and every one—then hug them all…

Critters

As I traveled northward this morning towards the Big Horn Mountains I viewed the southern chain in sunlight with new accumulations of snow while further to the North the mountain chain was hidden behind slate-gray clouds that bespoke of early snow. I arrived at my first service call in Dayton, Wyoming, at the base of the northern chain, and it was raining and cold. I talked with the customer and she told me that I could utilize the one door at the side to exit and enter, to service the water softener and reverse osmosis unit located within the laundry room.

She also asked that I be sure not to let her cats outside, but that I could leave the outer door open with the inner door remaining closed. I said I would be most careful not to let any of her cats out. She said she would be out in the garden covering her plants for the upcoming winter storm. I was working on the reverse osmosis when I looked down and saw one long-haired cat just outside the door in the rain. Now, I'm not a "cat person"—but I dropped everything I was doing and using my best cat-coaxing charm finally caught the cat and put the critter back inside the house and closed the inside door. I honestly could not remember the cat following me from inside the house to where I was working in the laundry room.

I went back to work and had started on the water softener when I looked down and the same critter was outside the door again. I quickly chased after the cat and once again caught it. Again I took the animal back inside the house and closed the same door again. I then began to look around to see just where the critter was getting out—but could not detect any opening. The first time I was sure the feline had walked directly behind me and slithered through the door. The second time I was sure the critter knew of an opening that I had not yet discovered. I am careful of the customer's wishes—especially concerning their pets. I don't need a phone call back to the office about me being abusive or not caring about their animals. So I'm always careful to respect their wishes.

I went back to work again and in fifteen minutes the cat was outside the door with me chasing after it in the rain. It was fast approaching its limit of nine lives. But I caught it again—with perhaps less "cat charm" that the previous two attempts. Again, I put the critter back inside—still wondering how in the heck this cat was getting outside each time, and knowing that the customer was going to skin my hide when she found her cat all wet from the rain.

About twenty minutes later the customer appeared in the laundry room and asked me to please not let the long-haired cat into the house as it was an outside cat. I said, "Ma'am—I've been putting the cat inside because I thought she was getting out". The customer said that she had been putting the cat outside and couldn't figure out how it kept getting inside. Being careful on service calls can drive one insane at times. Here I'm doing my best to please the customer and she's wondering just what the heck is wrong with me. We both had a good laugh on this one.

As I drove back South this afternoon through the rain and over a hundred miles to go, I thought about all the crazy things in life we encounter. I found it easier to relax my mind instead and view the mountains below the slate-gray clouds…Critters!

Perseverance

The Army taught me many things about life. But the single thing that remains with me to this day is that of "Perseverance". We all share this trait to some degree I suppose, but the Army taught it in a way that remains with me always. From Basic Training, to Advance Training, Noncommissioned Officer Course, Advance Noncommissioned Officer Course, Officer Candidate School, Officer Basic Course, Officer Advance Course, and Great Leaders—all of these taught me "Perseverance".

Many times I wondered if I would break, fall out, pass out or just die. On some occasions the "Pucker Factor" was high indeed. I found out early on that the difference on my making it while others didn't was pure mind-set. I gutted it out when others quit. I started out at a late age when I enlisted in the Army. Perhaps that gave me an edge on maturity that others younger than me didn't have yet. Now I'm not so sure that age is any longer a benefit—I'm not what I once was. But I did come to recognize that for every tough attempt at what might seem the impossible, and that in the end resulted in mission accomplishment, I grew just a bit more in mental outlook and "Perseverance".

I can still relive those times facing a new unknown, facing fears and having my own doubts questioning my process as I negotiated another tough obstacle. I also remember the ones who went by the wayside—and know that I too felt as they did when they lost it. Each day in one's life brings something new, something different, and sometimes a new crises that demands immediate attention and a decision. It's life's lessons and the great folks in our lives that bring to us the gifts that help us to not only endure, but to overcome. For each victory and defeat makes us stronger in some form or another. I have learned that "History" is hindsight.

The decisions we make on a daily basis with the facts and resources we have available at that time should not cause us grief in later life, but they do just the same. The "what ifs", "I should have done that", "if only I had known"—all cause us to think if the action and the path taken at the time were the right decisions. Truth is…we all make mistakes, sometimes serious ones. But we all make good decisions too in our lives. The difference is how we handled the bad decisions—and realizing that just possibly those were the ones that led to the good decisions. I call that "Perseverance". And keeping the Faith.

Grandfather Stevenson

Grandfather Stevenson was a remarkable man. He graduated in the first dental class from Indiana University and was the only still practicing dentist from that class when he finally retired. His mannerisms and respect for the individual still bring fond memories of his good nature. Even when sitting in the dentist's chair and eyeing that long needle going towards my gum line he was able to put me at ease simply by stating "This is going to sting a little". It still hurt, but that was okay because he was my Grandfather.

He loved to play golf, and was a wonderful fisherman. Wednesdays and Sundays would find him on the golf course. Winters he would venture to Florida for deep sea fishing, while some summers he would fly to some unknown lake in Canada where he fought with the Northern Pike and Walleyes. The reason he was the only practicing dentist from his class was because of his heart. He was kind and attentive to others when his classmates had "specialized" in certain fields of dentistry, made their fortunes, and retired early in life.

Grandfather Stevenson always wanted to know how you were doing, what interests and hobbies you had and took genuine interest in the events in your life. The main reason I succeeded in graduating from college was that I didn't want to disappoint him. At the low times in life he could bring you up on your feet again, simply by sharing time with you through discussion and exchanging thoughts. He made one feel positive about oneself. Grandfather always had a way of turning the conversation away from him and towards you. In many ways he was lacking in world affairs—what you received from him was not current events but down-home honesty. He honestly didn't know what a loaf of bread cost, could be taken on any quick-rich scheme, but overlooked the corruptness of the world about him.

A business man he was not. But a man of business he was—and the best. His patients always received the same care and treatment, whether rich or poor, no matter if they paid him on time or not. Their dental concerns were first and foremost his concern. And if he played golf on a Sunday morning instead of going to church it was only because the Good Lord knew who the Saints were on this earth of his, and allowed them the opportunity to relax once in awhile, playing golf or just fishing.

This world of ours today is filled with folks that are out for the almighty dollar, who place job before family, whose social life is more important than real friendships, and who jump on the next fast-moving wagon bound for new riches and fame. Rarely do we meet someone who has the time to really listen to us and who can make us feel better about ourselves and the lives we live. But when we chance upon that one individual who shows us a special interest and kind heart, attentiveness and real concern in how we're doing, the world becomes what it should become—caring.

The "sting a little" is just that…a little. We depart with a unique experience and a different outlook on life.

One Small Place

Golden leaves flickering in a slight breeze and covered with morning rays. Frost upon the brown grasses and trees, radiating glistening diamonds of light. Easy rolling hills that blend with the sky above. Overhead, a formation of geese heading south, their formation twisting as they align themselves on their leader. At this small place nestled beneath the hills and enclosed as if designed by the Master Gardner himself, the trees shield from view the Mule Deer browsing on the fall grasses. Fused hues and cautious movement make the buck almost invisible. Mixed within the various shades and colors of foliage appear old weathered buildings, now almost nondescript and as much a part of the scene as the deer.

Human habitation no longer exists at this site—departing long ago when either the climate no longer worked for those who lived here or other opportunities in other regions of the land became available. What sort of voices filled this area at one time? What were the hopes and dreams of those who lived here? What thoughts filled their minds as they went about their daily chores? Did he or she pause briefly at times, looking about, searching the landscape? And what one event became the reason for exodus? If those Pioneers still live, do they think about those days when they lived here, and have they ever returned for a brief visit since?

These impressions register in my mind as I travel slowly past this site, taking in all as I view this one place on earth among the expansiveness of the area. The middle of nowhere? Almost, but not quite. For long ago there was a different form of life here. What is missing now is its breath. So I watch the deer and wonder to myself, what generation are you Sir? How many of your ancestors grazed here and did they hear the voices and conversations of those people who made this their home at one time? The deer raises its head and looks at me as if to say that it understands my questions. And, as if in answering, lowers its head to continue grazing. I understand. The deer is one with Nature.

This magnificent creature does not fight the environment nor try to bend it to its own vision. It does not disrupt the land or take ownership. It realizes that in all of Nature, nothing stays the same forever. That life is a snapshot picture and that it soon changes, like the seasons—it comes and goes. The deer is content with that and understands. I round the next curve in the road in front of me, leaving behind this small place nestled beneath the hills and the message it shares with anyone willing to listen.

Trail West

I remember so many years ago when the teacher asked us kids in the classroom, "Okay, now we'll find out just what all of you did this Summer..." When my turn came around I was glad to tell them about my summer activities.

We had left our home back in Kentucky in April. It was during the rainy season and the roads were muddy and a lot of the wagons had trouble becoming mired in the stuff. We headed west as a small group of wagons with our sights set on Saint Louis, Missouri. Dad had said that this would be our departure point. It was wet and cold the whole trip to Saint Louis. After we reached Saint Louis and refitted our wagon and team of oxen we departed. I still remember the broad prairie spaces and the early spring. I was only ten years old then so I don't remember all of the landmarks that my Mother and Father spoke of on this journey of ours. But some I can still remember because I left my name engraved upon the rocks. I remember Chimney Rock and how it arose straight up out of the prairie and how red in color it was. I remember the North Platte River, Scott's Bluff and I remember reaching Fort Laramie where we stayed for a few days resting.

I remember crossing the North Platte River near a place called Fort Caspar and later in the summer reaching a large dome rock that everyone called Independence Rock because we made it there by the Fourth of July. I carved my name in that rock and dated it"1852". It was a high and windy place. Later we crossed a desert and reached a place they called the Continental Divide. My little sister died of cholera at that place and we buried her not far from the trail there.

It seemed that the world before me was always changing. I remember this time of the year when we reached the mountains of California and how delightful the colors were of the trees and mountain meadows. I also remember how cold it was becoming and that my Dad had said we were lucky to have made it through the mountains before winter closed in upon us. But along the trip west, the images that remain in my mind the most are those of the High Plains region. The unending herds of Buffalo, the clouds overhead and the shadows they cast upon the rolling landscape, the Antelope and the occasional Indian parties that came into view. I still recall the smell of canvas, wood and leather from the wagon, my Mother cooking over the open fire and the times I shared with the other kids on the trip. I remember the evenings around the fire at the end of a long day of walking. I remember the pain, suffering and sorrow that other families encountered.

But I also remember the good times we had when the weather was good and the trail was easy. We were between homes then. The old home in Kentucky we would never see again. And our new home yet to be seen. I lived in California for many years but finally ventured East again to the High Plains region and to a place that is now a state—Wyoming, my home.

I still remember the teacher asking "What did you do this Summer?" every time I venture out past the Red Desert area in southwestern Wyoming in search of my sister's grave, which I have never found. My response is, in my mind, that I had lived a lifetime that summer of 1852. So, what did you do this summer…?

Taking Care of Others

Shorter days and longer nights tend to cause me to withdraw. It's a seasonal thing I think. Summer's past and I see Old Man Winter walking down the road. Got to keep busy and not let my mind drift too far off course. Spent the day working on the truck—rotating tires, changing the oil, checking differentials and transfer case fluid levels, trying to grease the ball joints and inner/outer tie rod ends, but lacking the one tool I needed to accomplish the last task. Will have to find another grease adapter this coming week.

Country music playing on the radio and sitting in front of this machine, typing thoughts. Talking with Thomas and calling Amanda on the phone. Reading the local newspaper, my magazines and other literature about environmental concerns. And all the while wishing I were somewhere else—but where?

Companionship. Don't know how much you need that until you don't have it anymore. I can still laugh, but gave up crying a long time ago. Frustrations during the work week, and always trying to think things through, to no real conclusion. There are those times when I'm upbeat though—in a strange way. Took Thomas to Burger King Saturday night. Haven't been there for almost half a year. Hardly anyone there eating. But I watched a lady sitting at the table across from us with a sorrowful look on her face, staring at nothing. Eventually it all came together when her husband, who I had watched cleaning tables previously, sat down with her to have his supper. The only time they had together that evening was shared while he took a break from his job and the seven dollars an hour he was making.

I realized that I had been feeling sorry for myself until I watched them. I got to wondering too, how it is that in a country such as ours, there can be such a wide difference between the haves and the have-not. Oh, I know, we read about it occasionally—how the rich get richer, and the poor get poorer. But most of us never really look around ourselves at other ordinary folks. We're too busy, too ungrateful. Too wrapped up in our own lives to view the daily experiences of others. Imagine a life without "Hope", and no better tomorrow. A life of limited means, or emptiness. We left shortly after eating so I never saw how her visit went with her husband that evening.

My heart goes out to the people of this country who face a daily uphill challenge of trying to make things work out. Their lives make me grateful indeed for the many wonderful things that I have been fortunate in having in my life. But I would gladly give most of those things away if I could replace one of their sorrowful moments with true happiness. A smile, a certain light-heart, and most importantly—hope for the future.

We really need to be doing a better job of taking care of our own. I pause to listen to a country song on the radio, and wonder what I could be doing better for others.

Automotive

Sometimes overcoming the little things in life brings the greatest pleasures. Case in point—when working on my truck Saturday I encountered two grease fittings that I could not access on the inner tie rod ends. Regardless of how I turned the front wheels, jacked up the truck or approached those two fittings, I could not get the grease coupler on them. To make matters worse, it didn't look as if they had ever been greased even though the previous owner had the truck in for service on several occasions. I was frustrated to say the least, lying under the front end of the truck and spraying grease all over everything at each attempt. On top of that, every time I hit my head on the underside of the truck my head rebounded and I hit it on the ground below. Not bad—two bumps for the price of one!

So today I stopped at NAPA and described my dilemma to the counterman. He found a coupler which he assured me would work. Said they had sold a lot of those couplers for just that problem—so I bought it with skepticism. The guy was older than most fellows, but I've been doing automotive work for myself and others for thirty years now, and I had my doubts. Should have listened to my doubts as the thing didn't work worth a hoot!

So as I lay under the truck rubbing a new bump on my head, I got to thinking about the General Motors engineer who had designed this contraption. Who in their right mind would put grease fittings an inch away from the front drive shafts on a four wheel drive truck? Obviously they gave no thought to the poor smuck who had to grease them, and who obviously didn't because they couldn't get to them.

Now, one of the faults I have is that I do not like to be defeated. "Tenacity" is my middle name. I get something in my head that it should be one way and by golly it's going to be that way if I have to reform the whole world doing it. I've always enjoyed talking to other shade tree mechanics and sharing stories about our frustrations. I remember Al, who told me he was changing out the water pump on his old Chevy one time, using an open-end wrench which would slip off the bolt on the water pump housing resulting in skinned knuckles. The first time it happened he was pretty peeved. The second time it happened he was darn right irate. When it happened the third time he went ballistic. He took the wrench and knocked out the left headlight. Said it felt so good that he walked over to the right headlight and knocked that one out too. Then he wound up getting ready to throw the wrench through the windshield, but got a hold of himself finally. Then there was Lyn. His car would just all of a sudden die on him for no apparent reason. One day it died and Lyn jumped out of his car and kicked out his front headlight. Then he got back inside, and it started. He shifted into reverse so fiercely that he tore the gearshift knob off the shift lever, and had blood all over the interior. Well, I haven't gone that far.

So laying under that truck tonight I decided that the engineer that designed the grease fittings for those inner tie rod ends obviously needed a flashlight to see where he had his head. So I went back to another auto parts store and purchased some ninety degree grease fittings, took the straight ones out and replace them with the new ones. And they worked. I still looked like I had been working in the pit when I was done, grease all over my sleeves, fingers and the pavement—but the truck was finally greased. I had done battle with a company of grease monkeys. But I was smiling from ear to ear. I had beaten the machine once again, and put the automotive wiz-kids to shame once more.

Now the moral to this little story is, if at first you don't succeed—then change the rules. After all, they're not your rules but ones that someone else made up for you. Sometimes "Tenacity" can get you through when others things won't. I'm doing laundry tonight.

Cat's Farewell

Kittens. Something about the little felines make them adorable. When they're finally weaned and old enough to leave their mother they're still cute little balls of fur. So much energy and so independent, even when young. Constantly exploring and getting into everything that they shouldn't be getting into. Curtain climbers. It's hard to train a cat. I don't think it's because they don't have the mental capacity so much as it is that they are just going to do things their own way.

Butterball and Casper came from the same litter and we acquired them back in 1986. Later we acquired Mitzie, also a kitten. They were all with us back in the Army and Fort Knox days. They grew up with Amanda and Thomas there at Fort Knox. They gave me fits even then. I remember when we came west here to Wyoming back in 1989. A three day, two night ordeal from Kentucky. Our first night in the motel went okay, even though the cats were in their carriers during the trip and under a sedative. We let them out in the motel room that night and it was like a new confused freedom. (That was when I learned how to give a cat a pill.)

Our second night found us on the banks of the Missouri River and a motel that wouldn't allow pets. So we waited until dark and then I went down to the cars and covered the carriers with towels and sneaked them up to our second story room. Confused freedom once more, but they were out of their carriers for the night. We finally reached Gillette the third day and found a motel to live in for the next week and that allowed pets. The second week we found a house for rent outside of town and the cats finally had a home. It was October and cold, but they had a fenced back yard to roam in when they wanted to go outside. I adopted Tippy the summer of 1990 as a bouncing puppy but she was a outside dog and posed no threat to the indoor cats. January of 1991 we moved into a mobile home in town with the cats and Tippy. It was cold and snowy then. The cats stayed inside and Tippy remained an outside dog. Amanda and Thomas were growing up fast and during their childhood we acquired a few more critters for their enjoyment.

At one time we had the three cats, the dog, two parakeets, two hamsters and two gerbils. And yes, I did feel like a Zoo Keeper. But they were fun. Then there were the deaths of the hamsters, the gerbils, the parakeets. Amanda and Thomas grew older. Mitzie developed cancer that later claimed her life. She was a good cat. I loved the gerbils—especially Whiskers. I still remember holding Whiskers in my hand and feeling his last little feeble heartbeat when he finally expired. What wonderful characters, gerbils.

These days find me with old Butterball, Casper and Tippy. This weekend Amanda is arriving from Denver to visit her dad and brother, and to take the old kitties back with her to their last new home. Both cats have long since surpassed their nine-lives capacity. Butterball even ended up in the animal shelter one time when I had let him outside for a morning excursion and then forgot that I had let him out. Later that evening when everyone was looking for Butterball I was asked if I knew where he was. Duh—it finally dawned on me that I hadn't seen him since I let him out that morning. We looked all over the neighborhood but could not find him. Everyone was in tears, and I was frantic for losing him. Finally we called the animal shelter and, yes, they had a cat matching that description but we would have to wait until the following day to retrieve him, which we did.

Butterball had done time in the "Pokey", and I was in the Dog House. How these two cats have ever survived with my temperament is beyond me. I have put them into "airborne" status outside the front door on a couple of occasions. I have chased them around the house, and at two o'clock in the morning thrown a rolled-up newspaper down the hallway at whichever one was making a racket, waking me up from my sleep. I have cleaned the litter box and placed fresh food and water before them so many times that it has become a way of life. They have trained me well.

I have given them names such as "Critters", "Varmints", "Worthless Fur Balls"…and a few others. I have threatened to have Butterball stuffed when he expires and to turn Casper into a rug so that I can wipe my feet on his ornery hide every time I come in the house. Both look at me with complete understanding—"Yes, the man is totally nuts!" They have maintained their total independence and individuality all of these years—never bending to pressure from me, or anyone else.

Now that, Ladies and Gentlemen, is what I call "Character". As much as I have conducted cat-warfare against these two critters, I admire and respect the enemy's "Character". I know that I will miss them. They have become a part of my life whether they know it or not. And though I may not miss the cat hair, the racket, or the little surprising mine fields they plant in my way at times—I will miss them. They will be under excellent care with Amanda in Denver. I hope they will continue onward to even older age and happiness. Amanda will see to that. I grant them their freedom.

Birthday

I am a simple man for complex times. It's the simple things in life that make me most happy. This weekend was one of those simple times. Amanda and Thomas were here at home for my birthday. Simple things—like when Amanda went to the grocery before I got home from work on Friday and then fixed us all a burrito dinner. Or a bag full of miniature Snicker candy bars (I love Snickers!) Or a house filled with the laughter of my children. Laughing at me, or what the cats are doing, or what I said, or what they said.

Taking my daughter to a movie theater to watch a show and laughing all the way through the movie (*Meet the Parents*). Or fixing a simple problem on my daughter's truck for her. Getting a hug from my son or my daughter. Having my daughter laugh hysterically at my comment about getting old and me calling myself a "Crusty Old Bastard". Sharing a birthday lunch with Mike's (Amanda's boyfriend) parents and them picking up the tab. Watching the cats respond to my daughter's love. Or my son doing the dinner dishes for me.

Going to the gas station with my daughter at night and telling her to turn her lights on when driving home. "They are on, Dad." "No they aren't!" "Yes they are, Dad!" "No they are not!—Flick your bright lights on…See, the damn things aren't on!" "Yes they are!" "No they aren't!" And so on…

It's the simple things like saying "Goodnight—I love you" to my son and daughter before I go to bed at night, and then waking in the morning to find them sleeping while I get my coffee and go outside to watch the sun come up. Or having them all together this Thanksgiving and Christmas here in Wyoming. The house is quiet now—no cats, no son or daughter at home, just me and old Tippy. Better times will come again. Simple man waiting in complex times.

Time

I like it when things go according to intended plans. After all, that's organization. Most of us are more effective when our lives are somewhat structured. But what about the cost? What do we give up of ourselves when our lives are "structured"? What are the things that we miss out in our lives when we pursue a life that is structured and in accordance with the plans we have made for ourselves?

For instance, this weekend most of us will change our clocks to adjust to the shorter days. Fall—"Fall Back"; spring—"Spring Forward" the saying goes. This is in relation to the earth's rotation and the tilting on its axis to correlate with the seasons, thus the shorter days and longer nights. Time for the southern hemisphere to live it up for the summer. We've had our turn. "Time", as we know it has been calculated in calendars, seasons, and minutes. Its basis is our rotation around the sun and determines what day of the year it is, whether it's night or day, winter or Summer etc. Of course this is a highly structured, organized attempt of keeping track of "time". We also have the atomic clock to help us adjust to the slightest deviations and to get us back on course.

I think that is why I did so poorly in mathematics. You see, "mathematics" is an absolute science. When you did your math you either had the right answer, or it was wrong. No gray areas. I never have looked at life as an absolute, so I did poorly at math. I reasoned that there is nothing on earth that is absolute, nothing finite, and nothing definite. There are no two things exactly alike. Each has its own individual properties. Just as individual people are different from each other. "Twins" are not exactly alike—just similar.

Leave our Planet Earth, and you leave behind "time". Because time is an Earth value of measurement. Doesn't mean squat in space. Nor does the speed of light, which is faster than I can type this, you can be assured. So when all of my teachers were telling me that once again I did not have the correct answer to their absolute mathematical problem, I already knew that. Of course, with their education and credentials in teaching, they didn't have the correct answer either. It's like asking a question and the answer must either be "yes" or "no". I always thought that depended upon the question asked, how it was asked and what the expected answer was supposed to be.

Needless to say, I didn't like tests either. For every question asked, I could always find fault in the question itself. Like our own individual health, for instance. I doubt that on any given day we either feel exceptionally great, or exceptionally poor. It's more like a combination of the two extremes that determine if we have had a good day or a bad day. I can live within a "abstract" world—after all, I've done it for half a century. Half a century—hey that's 50 years. And with our mathematical wizards they should be able to tell me exactly when that point in time occurred—but they can't. At what point in our lives are we "born"?

No, I'll stay with the abstract. I came into this world with nothing and I'll leave this world the same way. I've asked the many forms of wildlife that I have encountered throughout the years, "What time is it?" and I always received the same response—"What is time?" Furthermore—what does it matter? One cannot control time, cannot keep time, cannot lose time—and I've know some folks who can't tell time. But that's okay too. This reminds me…it's time to go.

Drivers

There's something about some drivers' mentality that continue to amaze me when I'm driving around this town of ours. Oh, I know we all have encountered our fair share of driverless vehicles that appear out of nowhere intent on ruining our peaceful existence. These last few nights when I've been on the way home from work I've had one pickup try to slam into the side of my truck and one who was determined to make my rear bumper my front bumper.

Now, I'm not what one would call an aggressive driver, until I encounter someone with the personality of a rock. It seems that lately there are more and more vehicles on auto-pilot these days. Perhaps I am over-sensitive on how I'm driving and more critical of others who are "driving" lacks anything closely resembling control of their vehicle.

I think it has something to do with genetics. At one time in the far past all we had to do was put a foot in the stirrup, swing up on the horse and touch the flanks—and we were on the way. I grew up that way on the farm and later during my cowboy days. Never had to worry about if your "lights' worked or not—didn't have brake lights, head lights or turn signals. Never had to scrape a windshield in the middle of winter, or wait until the defroster was warm enough to see out of the glass. Didn't have to worry about how much fuel you had on board or if your bakes worked. No worry about bald tires (maybe a thrown shoe), seat belts or a horn. Never had to adjust a seat (maybe a cinch strap), or a rear-view mirror. What debris you found on the road your horse either stepped over or went around. If it got icy out you slowed down because who wanted to wear a horse on one's back. Of course, sometimes the horse had a mind of its own, but as its rider you had ultimate responsibility and control over the animal. You didn't need "horse" insurance to ride, or uninsured horse-rider insurance to cover you just in case some other rider plowed into you (which rarely happened). And I never received a recall notice from some horse factory telling me to bring my horse in or I'd violate my horse warranty (which I didn't have either).

In the Army Cavalry the horse was replaced with Armor, but the old cavalry concept still prevailed when I was with the Cavalry. Simply stated, the three pre-requisites, in descending order were—"Horse, Saddle, Rider". That meant that one first took care of the Horse (so you would be able to move when required), then the Saddle (which consisted of all the equipment necessary in maintaining the Horse), and lastly the Rider (You). Nowadays it's just the opposite—if done at all. First and foremost, today's drivers think first of themselves. Secondly, they might look at their vehicle's equipment (Oh, I have a flat tire, no oil in the engine, and I'm out of antifreeze, again. I wonder if I have a leak somewhere.) And coming in dead last is the vehicle itself. I've seen a lot of two-hundred dollar cars with three-thousand dollar stereo systems. (Actually, I've heard more than I've seen.)

Of course nowadays you see folks who can't drive at all, talking on cell phones, smoking in their cars or trucks, or yakking to their passengers, while maintaining eye-to-eye contact with them. The fact that there is another world just outside their front windshield doesn't even enter into their thought process. But again, that's genetics. Its origin is once again with the horse, when there were no cell phones, you could still holler and be heard, flip your cigarette onto the ground, and turn in the saddle and carry on a conversation with your riding partner and let your horse go its own way. That too, is why drunk driving remains a problem—genetics! One left the bar somewhat sober to place your left foot in the stirrup, swing on up on your horse and, if you were lucky, stay in the saddle. If you did make it down the road and passed out you at least had a chance of coming around when you hit the ground. And then there was the opportunity to try and catch your horse, and attempt the process again. After awhile you figured out that the only one getting abused in this process was you, so you cut down on your consumption the next time you visited the saloon on horseback. There are few second chances for this stupidity nowadays.

But still—it's genetics. That's the problem I have driving around town. Whereas, I have "bridged" the two separate worlds of past and present, most of today's "drivers' have no concept of how they got where they are when they are trying to make me "history". So, when I start feeling depressed about the driving techniques of our town's drivers, and the fact that they have lost their true riding heritage, I take a trip to Denver to visit my daughter, and to further appreciate our total lack of sanity in these parts.

Veteran's Day

Cold. Very Cold. It had been a long day that started at first light. Before the sun had arisen in the eastern sky the bullets had zinged past and smacked into the very ground above his head, sending dirt flying in all directions. That, and the roar of cannon shells exploding all around. Huge columns of smoke tracing from the ground upward after impact, the earth shaking beneath his body as each round sought a target, and took the life of another dear friend.

The trench where he lay was in ruins and was characteristic of the rest of the war-torn battlefield of craters, broken concertina wire, and bodies lying in all matter of distorted shapes and positions. Cold, very cold now that night had once again come upon him. He thought of his family back home in the States—his mother and father, sisters and brothers. What might they be doing this 11th day of November? Was it so cold there as well? He had done his best in fighting for freedom, his homeland, and his family. But what saddened him presently was that so many of his fellow soldiers had done the same, yet were no longer here. Doughboys. Guys just like himself, who had already departed from these trenches and this hell, on their way somewhere other than the home they had left behind. They had all signed up together—patriotism ringing in their ears and on every word they had spoken together.

That was a long time ago. Since then it was only the kinship, the esprit de corps, that they share together, that kept them as one. And now that was gone as well. Quiet, very quiet tonight. No cannons, no gunfire—nothing but a occasional flare in the sky overhead. There had been rumors that this war was coming to an end—he had heard them all before, yet nothing had happened in the past to prove them so. Rumors. It didn't matter now. He knew he would not be going home. His shattered leg and arm, his blood-coated and muddied uniform told the whole story. And the cold—so very cold now. Only he, lay in this trench tonight. But his thoughts stretched outward, forever. Would any of this matter in the years to come? At least it was peaceful tonight. Was it peaceful in other places along the front line? What had he accomplished as a soldier, as a son, a brother? He would never know, to be sure. But that did not matter any longer. He had done his very best. May God grant mercy on his soul.

It must be close to eleven o'clock tonight. Odd—the eleventh hour of the eleventh day of the eleventh month. Eleven was perhaps a good number. Cold—so very cold. So tired. Time for sleep—a deep, deep sleep.

Farewell

Today was a heart-breaking day for me. Karla loaded all of her items into the U-Haul trailer that she is towing behind her car and left for Indiana this morning. Thomas stayed home from school today to help his Mother. I had a service call in the neighborhood and decided to drive by our house and noticed that Thomas was home and Karla's car and U-Haul were there. I stopped in to say goodbye to her since I had not yet seen her since she had been back in town these last few weeks. I gave her a warm embrace and told her that I loved her.

Thomas told me tonight that she left fifteen minutes after I left. I'm glad that she was able to take all of the items she wanted to take with her and just hope that she has a safe trip on the way back. It's a good two-and-a-half days to get back to Columbia City and to her Mother's. I didn't think she should be pulling that trailer behind her car because I thought it would be too heavy for the car, but she was determined anyway. At least I was able to see her before she left Wyoming. If I had been fifteen minutes later I would have missed her. Even though she has been on the road for almost eleven months now I always knew she could come back here anytime she wanted between stores. That, and the fact her items were still here. Even this last week when I didn't see her because she would pack during the day while I was at work and leave before I arrived home afterwards, she still had her items here in boxes at least. I knew that she would be back to do more.

But now all of those things are gone, and so is she. There was nothing that I wanted for myself so I had told her beforehand to take whatever she wished. I still know nothing as to when her attorney will have the divorce finalized—I guess he will let me know. I never asked, but just did as she wished me to regarding any paperwork. Tonight I took Thomas out for supper. He is emotionally stable, but I know that he hurts too. I am so glad that he is here with me. I am fifty-one years old and have spent over half of my life with one woman—my wife and the mother of our children. I think back over all of those years—the good times and rough times.

But somehow I can't remember the bad times. Only the good moments together and the love shared. I have been truly blessed to have had such a wonderful woman in my life, though she may not feel the same way about me. I don't know that I'll ever see her again—or that she would want me to see her. But my thoughts and blessings will always be with her. Back when we were dating I would draw her pictures of Butterflies and leave them as folded notes in her area at work. I would write that "Butterflies Are Free" on the notes because I felt that she was my Butterfly and that I would never keep her from her freedom. I still felt that way even after we married. Today, before I left for work I left a small box on the kitchen table that contained the wedding ring she gave me and the corsage that I wore at our wedding, with a note attached stating:

Karla—

My wish for you is that of happiness. Butterflies are free.

Love, Ron

I am thankful that she took the box with her.

Insurance Exam

Having worked the Friday after Thanksgiving, even though it was a paid holiday, entitled me to take today off from work instead. I woke up at three o'clock this morning (odd, that on days off I don't need the sleep) and took the dog out for the day. I had a long drive ahead of me, as I was heading for Casper, Wyoming. The purpose of my excursion to Casper was to take the state insurance licensing examination for becoming a health and disability insurance agent. As I had received no formal schooling or classes and had to study for the examination on my own, the "unknown" that awaited me as to whether I could pass the state examination weighed upon my mind.

As I departed from home at six o'clock the sun was just breaking the horizon. I took Highway 50 south out of town. Now, when I drive any distance unaccompanied in the dark, I always make preparations for the trip. This trip was no exception with the usual requirements in case of a winter storm, bad roads, possible mechanical breakdowns, etc. I took my CDs along because, even though I'm on caffeine "high" from all of the coffee I have consumed, it's always enjoyable to have some music to listen to. My selection this morning for music was the sound track from the movie "Braveheart". If you haven't seen the movie, you should. If you haven't listened to the sound track, you're missing an important element in life.

As the glow increased in the eastern horizon, and the pink hues brightened the road ahead, the Scottish music swelled the interior of the truck cab and I departed earthly existence and headed for the heavens above. (The truck remained on the highway, though.) What a way to begin a day—driving through early dawn with the stars still above, the road ahead to an unknown, and the music lifting my spirits. I gazed out upon the landscape, watched as a large herd of mule deer grazed alongside the highway, and I was the only driver out there in the middle of nowhere. In all of the years spent with Nature, and watching the days turn to nights and back again to days, the two most enjoyable times for me are dawn and dusk. Those are the times that, while the rest of the world sleeps, one can enjoy the company of the wildlife and the changing of the worlds. I've seen something different at every sunrise and every sunset—no two are the same.

I arrived in Casper and still had time for breakfast before the examination, so I stopped at JB's and had a omelet and more coffee. The day had begun on more than one "note", and I had enjoyed every one of them. The "impressions" that always remain in one's mind are the fleeting ones—those one-time events that can never be duplicated again. It was one of those times while driving this morning.

Oh—I did pass the state insurance licensing examination. Almost forgot, while I was enjoying life.

Election Time

Every time I start feeling low, I stop to consider how those poor voters are coping in Florida with this last Presidential election. Then, I feel so much better, and grateful, that I can read and write, and that I don't have to worry about some court deciding if I voted the right way or not. I like politics because those sorry politicians make me feel human. It must be a living hell not to be in touch with anyone or anything around you.

Last year I became a Life Member of the Sierra Club. This year I became a Life Member of the National Rifle Association. The fact that each organization holds opposing views towards who should be President doesn't bother me in the least. After all, my beliefs towards the environment are no different than those pertaining to the beliefs that each individual has the right to protect and defend themselves from governmental tyranny or aggressive individuals. I would no more relinquish one belief than I would the other. So what if the organizations that I am a life member of can't figure it out. I've made a statement.

I see talent in the political arena all of the time. Al Gore can do more with chads than Clinton could ever do with cigars. Obviously Georgie Bush, Jr. never followed his dad's example when his dad gave up his membership in the NRA because of the jack-booted governmental thugs. Georgie, I believe, is pro-gun. He just can't shoot straight. He reminds me of a little kid. Al Gore, on the other hand, reminds me of a juvenile delinquent. He doesn't get his way and he either wants to change the rules or start the game over.

I'm sure glad there are no real contestants for the Presidency—I would feel bad then. There have been real contestants in the past for the Presidency, but of course they never stood a chance. I voted for Ross Perot in two elections. He wasn't any worse than the two present candidates—at least you knew where he stood. That's why he didn't have a chance.

To be a politician one must lie to everyone and be truthful to no one. Sure, Florida has a nice climate in the winter. Who wouldn't want to be wading along the ocean beaches when back home in Old Wyoming the truck won't start, the water lines are frozen, the power lines are snapped from all of the ice, and the roads are closed again because of the latest snow storm. The difference is of course that here in Wyoming we can read all about the latest news and weather in the local paper, whereas in Florida they're still trying to get past the comics.

Jackalopes

A few years back when camping out in the Grasslands I had spent the entire day trekking quite a distance, exploring numerous terrain features and encountering a variety of wildlife. At the close of this one particular day, I had finished drinking my last cup of coffee out under the stars and had thrown the last log on the fire for the night when I finally decided to retire for the evening. As I lay down, the many things I had happened upon that day crossed my mind. I was puzzled by a trail I had come across that had the many prints of what I thought were large rabbits. I had never seen such a sight before. Even though I knew there were numerous jackrabbits in the area, I had never seen so many prints in file and for such a distance.

As I drifted off into sleep I was awakened suddenly by a low rumble that seemed to come from ground level. As I usually do when awakened suddenly in the wilds by a strange noise, I simply lay still with my eyes fully adjusted to the dark and my hand resting on my revolver. I carefully rolled over and peered about me at ground level when to my astonished eyes I caught sight of a great number of critters in the moonlight jumping about in all directions immediately around my camp site. I cautiously reached for my Mag light and aimed the flashlight with my one hand while taking aim with my revolver.

I depressed the flashlight switch and immediately the area came alive with light and furry bodies. Hundreds of little eyes shined in the light, frozen for the moment as they gazed intently at me. As my prone body was at ground level, I was startled to see so many creatures that seemed to tower above me in the light. But what immediately caught my attention was the fact that, as I scanned this small herd with my light beam, each and every one of these furry creatures had what appeared the body of a large jackrabbit, but with antlers. Fully alert now, I realized that I was in the midst of a large herd of Jackalopes! I remained completely still, knowing that the least amount of movement on my part would send these magnificent creatures into a stampede that would completely overwhelm me and destroy my campsite. Finally, in what seemed like hours, but I'm sure was only minutes, the herd began to move away with the sound of a low rumble as they continued to jump out of my campsite, on their way to who knows where.

I switched off the flashlight and rolled over onto my back and let out a sigh of relief. Once again I had survived a near disaster with Nature by almost being trampled to death. As I slowly drifted back into slumber I was grateful that at least I was out here on the ground during the warm weather, and not out camping in the middle of winter. Whereas I don't relish the cold and sleeping on the ground in the middle of winter, my biggest fear during the cold months is that of being over-run by the venomous species of the Snowsnake. Now, that's another story…

Seasons

I believe that "seasons" are best enjoyed by those who do not suffer through them. Take winter for example. There are those snow-buffs that truly enjoy the snow and cold for recreational purposes. They like skiing, snowboarding, snowmobiles, ice fishing and I'm sure numerous other activities. Granted, there is a spectacle when the sun shines on frosted tree limbs or the snow crust breaks beneath warm feet on a short excursion. A white landscape is like a lunar landscape—surreal and different. But then there are those folks, like myself, who find themselves at times working outside during the winter months.

Today was one of those times, when I'm trying to lift and drain a two-hundred pound tank of resin and water in a fifty mph wind on a hill crest. I find the romance of winter disappearing quickly as the ice begins to coat my fingers and the wind chill doesn't mean anything because you can't feel your hands anyway. (I was wondering at the time why my fingers had transformed themselves into stumps.) I've cut myself in this kind of weather and never had to worry about bleeding to death because it froze before going anywhere. No bandage required. (Hurts like hell when you get thawed out though.)

No, I think that folks who enjoy a particular season do so because they have not suffered enough during that season. I like summer. Spring and fall are okay, but Summer I can live with. It might be due to age. So many old folks head for warmer climates like California, Florida or Arizona when they get older. Some stay there year around. But I like summer because I don't mind sweating. Freezing—I do mind. Sometimes I wish I was like my dog, Tippy. In the Spring I could shed my coat, and in the Fall I could grow a new one. (At my age I can still grow hair, but usually in the wrong places. I have definitely lost hair in the places I shouldn't have lost it.)

I can't imagine living anywhere where there aren't seasons. Even here in Wyoming we at least have two seasons—winter, and Road Construction. But without seasons to live through each year I believe one would lose the appreciativeness of the more harsh seasons. What good is summer with nothing to compare it to? I've always thought it sad that a large number of wildlife mortality usually occurs in the early spring. Having survived a fierce winter, many of the critters have few reserves remaining when the last of the spring snow storms hit, and they just die. To have endured for so long and then to lose it all in the end.

So, that's why I am so appreciative of winter. I know that if I can get through winter then all I have to do is be careful of spring. And then it's summer again. That's what I told my stumpy fingers today—"Hang in there fellas, summer is on the way!"

Bird Feeder

I had a warm thought today, but for the life of me I can't remember what it was. My mind froze up, literally. Several weeks ago I placed a new bird feeder outside and filled it with birdseed. But the birds never used it. In prior years they always congregated around the wooden bird feeders that I had place outside for them. Since this new bird feeder was plastic I was of the opinion that I had wasted my money on its purchase, even though the wooden feeders took a real beating in the winter weather. I did notice that some birdseed had disappeared from the feeder in the last few days or so, which I thought may have been due to the wind blowing the feeder around.

At any rate, yesterday I filled the bird feeder full, due to the extreme cold and snow. Last night, the bird feeder was still untouched, but I brushed the snow off it at any rate. When I went outside this morning before the sun was up it was minus twelve degrees. I guess it broke the zero mark sometime today—little consolation for the minus fifteen degree temperature we're having tonight. I am grateful that the wind is not blowing (unusual for Wyoming) during this arctic weather.

Today, while outside on my many excursions I noticed that my feet felt like stubs. When I got home tonight I listened to the wood steps and the wood shed popping in the frigid air outside. I brought the dog in earlier than usual, but she wants to go outside with me whenever I go out. Animals somehow adapt more readily than humans to extreme weather changes. (I guess I would too if I didn't know how to start a fire.)

In the Army I had a good friend and Special Forces Officer who would say, "You don't have to practice to be miserable". Somehow, that has always stuck with me, especially now as I move out of adolescence into adulthood. I have found out that, after awhile when you've been subjected to below freezing temperatures at the minus fifteen or so that a few more degrees downward really don't matter at all, since you're already miserable. I can't distinguish degrees of suffering—either you're suffering or you're not.

I've had frostbite a couple of times—you know when it happens to you because you can't feel anything in that area, until you thaw out. I think of frostbite as just another burn, from the other extreme, and treat it accordingly—carefully. When I came home tonight I noticed that the ground beneath the bird feeder was covered in seed, and bird tracks all over the place. The bird feeder was almost completely empty. Ah, my fine feathered friends have finally come home to Papa.

I refilled the feeder again tonight, pleased that even the birds know that you don't have to practice to be miserable. Except, now I have created a welfare program for the little ones. If it keeps them alive until spring, that will be fine with me.

Wyoming Trucks

To get the best buy on a used vehicle you must travel to Wyoming. It is there, and a few other Western states, that one will find the best of used vehicles—especially trucks or other four-wheel drive vehicles. Let's run down the list of a few things to look for when shopping around for that perfect truck.

First of all, it's got to have four-wheel drive—that works. A two-wheel drive truck in Wyoming makes about as much sense as a screen door on a submarine. It just gets you into something that you can't get out of. A car, even front-wheel drive, doesn't have the ground clearance and can't get you anywhere seriously off-road. Winter driving in Wyoming is nearly always off-road, even when one is driving on the streets.

Next, there should be an electrical cord hanging outside the front hood or grill somewhere. That tells you that there is a engine block heater somewhere under the hood. That way when it's twenty below zero (or less) you can plug in your truck so it will start in the morning. (No matter how well-tuned your vehicle is—it won't start at thirty below zero. It's called the fuel/air mixture thing.) The battery should be heavy-duty with more cold-cranking amps in the thousand-plus range. (Cold-cranking amps go down as the temperature decreases. An adequate battery in fair weather becomes two AA batteries in the severe cold.) Tires on the truck have deep treads. Highway radials just put you in the ditch faster.

When looking beneath the possible purchase of your vehicle, you will see little rust on the frame and exhaust system. That tells you that it is a true Western vehicle—not a salt-eaten Western wanabe look-alike truck. Windshield wipers will be winter blades—the type that look like squeegees they use to clean store front windows. (Open frame wipers just hold the ice and snow preventing the wipers from cleaning the windshield.) Inside the truck you will find full-size floor mats (if carpeted) made of rubber. Carpet floor mats hold moisture and in cold weather add moisture to the inside of the vehicle's windows. You should try the heater on full blast to be sure that you can roast hot dogs on the defroster. If it won't roast a hot dog then it's not a Wyoming truck, and it won't keep you warm either.

The bed of the truck will either have a rubber bed mat or a full piece of plywood to keep items from sliding around. A wrap-around bed liner is useless as it just allows whatever cargo in the bed to slam from one side to another when cornering. Looks nice—but is useless. Next, there should be some tire chains either in the cab or in the bed of the truck. If you have a four-wheel drive truck then the tire chains go on the front tires—not the rear tires. That's where the pulling power is when in four-wheel drive—especially when you're trying to get out of the snow bank you just drove into.

On the front of the truck there are at least two functioning headlights and two auxiliary lights of some type. The auxiliary lights are usually driving lights not fog lights, and usually mounted lower to the ground. They allow one to see the ruts in the snow when sides of the road are invisible while driving. Back inside the cab you should find a sleeping bag, some dry food, water, matches, candles, a cell phone etc. Back outside the truck will be at least one tow hook—usually two, with a tow rope or snap rope somewhere inside the cab. Should be a first aid kit in there somewhere too. Sometimes you'll find a scoop shovel and bags of sand in the bed of the truck, for digging out.

And lastly, there should be a few empty beer cans in the bed of the truck. That tells you that the driver is conscientious about not littering the public highways. Happy Winter Motoring!

Sayings

Everyone has low periods in one's life. Then, there are those times when, for no apparent reasoning, the blessings we have received in our lives enter into our thoughts. Such is that special time tonight as I reflect on those many blessings in my life. I've been through personal hell more times than I want to remember, but I have also been more than fortunate in my lifetime.

I began life as an infant where my birth mother detested my crying and would throw me into the crib, and later threw me away for adoption because I was too much trouble. What a blessing—to be thrown into my adoptive parent's loving home.

So many words remain with us from our earlier days when we were growing up—words from parents and grandparents alike. On the subject of "Pride" I was taught that, "Pride goes before the fall". In the arena of physical "Strength", my father always said that, "Dynamite comes in small packages". Grandmother said, "No matter how poor you are, you can always afford soap". (I really wasn't that dirty as a kid.) At one time when I was feeling selfish and unloved, my father told me, "If we didn't love you, we wouldn't have you". Another time, Grandmother told me that, "All the riches in the world won't buy you health". She also said, "Friends may come and go, but your family is forever". Mother was more direct when she would say, "You're going to get it when your dad gets home!" (She knew the art of delegated responsibility.)

But, all in all, it was more the way those and other phrases were expressed, and the particular situations that initiated such sayings, that have remained with me throughout the years. All were expressed with love and the intent of teaching a young rebel like me the finer aspects of life. And they stuck. "You can get more bees with honey than you can with vinegar."

Yes, I count my blessings and consider myself very fortunate to have had those "Teachers" in my life. A stubborn kid, who grew up on a farm and encountered life, from birth to death. When told to clean out the hog house, I responded that "I wasn't born to clean out hog houses!" (Of course, I now realize that the Almighty's intent for my being born will forever remain a mystery to me, and I will probably never know why I'm here.) I believe that life has a rhythm, and we either enjoy it's company or we are helplessly out of tune with what is around us.

So, if you're like me and have one of those days where, as I say, "Everything has gone to hell in a hand basket", just remember those forgotten words that you grew up with and that still have meaning in you life. I have had their words to live by, good health, and plenty of soap.

Snow Music

I watched as the wind took the snow, like a wave of sand over the dunes. There was a pattern of movement, twirling at ground level, then straightening, then flowing away from me as another wave took its place. The whiteness waltzed before my eyes, curving first one way then another. Wherever there appeared small vegetation that peeked above the chiseled drifts, the wind would wrap itself around each tiny obstacle of twig and leaf, depositing curving drifts, and then seeking another form of life further away. Occasionally blasts of wind would backwash in my direction and cover me with the soft, stinging moisture of snow. Clouds of white would rise from the ground and twirl about me taking my visibility with it. The sun blazed through the grainy mist—enhancing crystals of light and surrounding me with a bright shower of powder. Sparkling, cold, with melting moisture upon my face.

This is a time unlike any other season of the year. Nature's movement across open areas, where one can track her progress by the dancing snow. I thought of my days in the desert and how the sand would move the same way across the ground. Snow and sand—two extremes of Nature, both dancing in rhythm with each other, climates apart. And always, the wind conducting its symphony of rising and falling melodies in its musical score. I wish I could dance, like the wind does with the snow and the sand—harmony in movement and gracefulness in action. But I'm like the vegetation in the snow, unable to move—and so I must be content in observing the composer at work.

There goes another wave—chasing the previous one that just departed from me. Unending energy hurrying away to be replaced by a newer and different form of snow rapture. Some folks call these forms of movement "ground blizzards". I call them poetry. Ah, if I were a lad again, I would dance with the snow.

Resolutions

I don't hold much in the way of New Year resolutions. Basically, I have yet to adjust to the calendar world of mankind. To do that, I would have to adjust to the rigors of time as well. My kinship with Nature and the animal kingdom prevents me from structuring my life in accordance with time. Perhaps that is why I remain so young. Years mean nothing.

The "resolutions" that I have made in the past were done so while I was still a tadpole. As a Cub Scout and later as a Boy Scout, the "resolution" that had importance to me then and now was that I…"Would do my best, and do my duty, to God and my Country, and to obey the Scout Law". That pretty well covered it then. Oh, I know I could make some resolutions. I could give up an occasional nip of alcohol, or a casual smoke of the old pipe. I could lose weight and look like Gandhi. I could get some Rogaine or maybe Miracle Grow for my receding hair line. Too, I could use less descriptive adjectives in my conversations with the "rocks" I encounter from time to time. I could drive more defensively instead of offensively as well.

I could probably even say I was sorry for some past wrong that I did to someone and try to make it up to them—even if I thought I was right at the time I committed the offense. I could do a lot of things in the way of resolutions, but I won't. I value my health too much I guess. Doing without all of the vices and second-guessing my thought processes would drive me absolutely batty. I found out a long time ago that folks will view you for who you are, no matter how much polish you muster.

I don't consider myself any better in psychology than the next Joe, and can see through most farces as well as anyone. I admit that at times I can be outspoken and somewhat blunt, leaving little doubt about what my true feelings are. I'm not so sure that is necessarily a fault. Making resolutions that one can't keep, is a fault. I sure would enjoy doing things right all of the time and being correct in everything that I do. But that would have to be done in accordance with my standards because if such actions were done by other folk's standards I couldn't possibly do them right or correctly. I'm better off just being who I am, I guess.

For those of you who do make resolutions and keep them, my hat is off to you. You obviously have found the meaning of life that I am still in search of. I never begrudge one the attempt of improving oneself. And of course, I try not to laugh too loudly at resolution failures. I usually greet the New Year by sleeping. After all, I came into this world asleep, before being awaken and shot across the delivery room. Maybe the only resolution I'll try to keep is to get more sleep. That and keeping the Scout Oath. Happy New Year!

A New Year

My message at the close of this year is to try and get along with others. I am particularly at fault in this area. I really don't enjoy being the cause of consternation or upsetting other folks. I like to "blend" in so that I am not disturbing or cramping other people and their lifestyles. I believe strongly that we do best in areas where the only "pressures" are our own self-inflicted criteria. But I also believe that now and then one must stand firm in one's own beliefs.

Case in point—Tonight after taking Thomas to dinner at Humphrey's I decided to stop in at the Good Times package liquor store to get some beer. Now, I know that there are some folks who would disapprove of this decision, so to alleviate you of any stressful moments regarding this action; I'll just say it was my decision and not yours. At any rate, as I tried to enter the parking lot, a van with California plates decided to stop for no apparent reason thus blocking my access to the parking lot and leaving me sideways on Highway 59 with oncoming traffic. I made the decision to go around him on the left side and get off the highway rather quickly.

I entered the store when this same driver also entered the store while I was at the cash register. He made some comment about a driver of the red truck outside. I told him that I had a red truck and "Why?" he wanted to know. He said that maybe I should slow it down. And I told him that maybe next time he'll get into the parking lot and allow me to get off the highway. Another fellow next to me at the counter said for me not to worry about the other guy, and I told this fellow "Hell, I'm not worried about him!" The California driver was fuming. I got my purchase and left the store.

Now this California man was a lot bigger than me physically, but I didn't care—I was ten feet tall and ready to dance him around the room. I don't like rudeness nor do I enjoy someone who thinks that their existence on this earth is for everyone's enjoyment. But, again I am straying. When I think about it, I've had a tough year this year and I'm not going to oblige some California ego.

But you see—all of that is wrong. What's wrong about it is that I didn't "blend" and just become another peaceful person. And that's what is wrong with our world today—not the blending part, but getting along peacefully with others. I could have made this another of my "Considerations" but for all of my faults (that I am willing to share with others) I think it more appropriate to just make it a message instead. Search out the good in everything. Help those that are in need. Overlook the transgressions of others. And above all, seek "Peace" in all that you may encounter in the New Year.

Melody of Darkness

Melody of darkness. That's what I call the night. Sitting on the back step and gazing into the night sky, or standing with my back to a dying campfire—its illumination flickering shadows across the sage around me. Total blackness with the millions of diamonds in the sky as the only source of light, is fine also.

I have never feared the night, but have been fascinated by what I cannot see. The world as we know it, is not the same at night. Sounds are different—more pronounced and with greater clarity. A rock that descends from a overhanging shelf and explodes like gunfire on the rocks below. Rock smoke barely discernible in the distance where the noise originates. Some small creature scurrying in front of me, dodging the ground vegetation and hurrying past. A cool wind that causes me to turn my back to it. Occasionally, I see a shooting star with its tail of light, as it arcs in the horizon and descends from my sight. The needles of the pines sing in the wind all night, sometimes suffocating other night noises. I have walked across the prairie at night by myself, carefully negotiating the various rocks and grasses. When the moon is full on the prairie it is as if it were daylight. I can read my watch without using a light and can see across the valley to the trees on the other side. The rutted trail become a highway in the moonlight.

Sometimes the mysterious becomes apprehension. Did that shadow move or was it just my eyes? I don't use a flashlight when I'm out on the prairie or in a mountain valley. I don't want others to know where I am and the flashlight beam only illuminates where one directs it. Peacefulness, is what darkness brings with it. The heavens are somewhat brighter in the winter months, but it's harder to maintain one's concentration with the cold. Ah, but the spring and summer skies are what the heavens were made for—lost in one's own thoughts. I have fallen asleep under a starry summer sky, with my eyes open, or so I thought at the time when I finally awoke. Sometimes, just having the loneliness is company.

Always, I regret that others are not able to share in the same experiences I enjoy. When I finally tally up my life functions at the end of this earthly existence, I know that in the final analysis I will find that the simple pleasures will indeed be my most cherished treasures. I do not fear death—for death is like the darkness, and is a fascination of what I cannot see. A melody.

Back to Work

Some days are better than others. It's what one does with the less-than-better days that make a difference at times. Last night, as I was sitting in a hotel room in Salt Lake City and preparing for another until-midnight study exercise, I got to thinking about what it was I was doing and where it was I was heading with my intentions of becoming an insurance agent. I still had a week and a half to go before I could even leave Utah, and when I did return to Wyoming, the District Manager had plans for me to be either in Glenrock or Sheridan for another week.

Attending classes "dressed up" in shirt and tie each day is not how I envision myself. I'm a blue jean, cowboy boot kind of guy. Memorizing a sales presentation word for word stifles my creativeness as well. The classes and the instructor so far had been excellent—the insurance policies being studied were exceedingly good policies. In fact, even the long hours in the classroom and the six hours in the evenings afterwards studying for the next day's assignment were fruitful, until last night. I couldn't concentrate—couldn't focus on the important facts that I had to remember for the next day's class.

As I searched for the problem to my dilemma I came to realize that I missed my home in Wyoming. I missed Thomas back there in Gillette—and would miss him even more after I returned and left again to either Glenrock or Sheridan for another week. I missed my dog, Tippy. I missed the scenery and the comforts of home. I missed my blue jeans and cow-kickers. I missed...me.

Where did I go and what did I become instead. Then, I realized that the real problem facing me and preventing me from concentration and focusing on my studies was that...my heart just wasn't in it. I was giving up everything for what...a better income and lifestyle? At what cost to me, personally? What is a dollar worth? How about sixty thousand of them, or a hundred thousand of them? Or more. And for what price?

I picked up the phone and called the instructor at his home and told him I was withdrawing from the course. Then I called the District Manager in Wyoming and told him the same thing. Next, I called my previous employer and I asked him if he still wanted me back at Western Water Conditioning. He was adamant—"Yes!" So I called the airlines next, and booked a flight from Salt Lake City to Gillette, and I arrived back home this afternoon. I went on over to see Ross at Western Water Conditioning and he, the book keeper and other technician were ecstatic to see me return. I go back to work in the morning—in jeans. I really did hit the ground running this time. Just in a different direction. Home.

Horses

Reading tonight's paper I ran across the old phrase, "There's never been a horse that can't be rode, there's never been a rider that can't be throwed". That phrase was captured in an article pertaining to internet hackers and a contest that was being run for them. I understood the terminology but had some trouble grasping the concept of how horses and computers were related in philosophy.

I was raised with guns, cattle and horses. We didn't have computers back then. I did have, and some say still have, a wild side to my nature. You could call it foolishness, or just plain stupidity when it came to horses on my part. I loved the creatures that taught me to fly like the wind. My Uncle Bob once told me in my youth that I was a natural horseman and born in the saddle. I considered that the highest of compliments. (Especially from an Uncle that was prone to ride a horse from beneath its belly when a cinch strap slipped on one occasion.) The neighbors—the Burns, at one time pastured a few of their horses on the old homestead. Among those was a black stallion that I had a certain fondness for. He was a little on the wild side and a few bricks short of a full load.

One day I decided to ride with the wind, and took a hankering to jump upon his back and hang onto his mane and let him have his way. And away we went—ass over elbows. After several minutes I found myself thrown and crushed inside a briar patch. Of course, this beautiful creature was still in tune with the wind, never looking back at his abruptly dismounted rider.

When I returned from Wyoming in 1968 I was a counselor for the YMCA summer camp at Flat Rock River in southern Indiana. The director placed me in charge of taming the ponies for the camp kiddies, and allowed me to work with a Tennessee walker that had thrown him and was just being plain stubborn. Now this was one beautiful horse. I guess the director figured that with my background of recent cowboy adventures and the fact that I was born in Kentucky—the land of beautiful horses and fast women, that I could manage this creature as well.

This magnificent horse was quite capable of flicking the bit from the back of its mouth to where he could clamp on it with his teeth, then going into auto-pilot. He put me into a tree more than once by backing into the branches then rearing up to try and brush me off on the limbs. I hung on because I had nowhere else to go. The director told me that this was one mean horse. I only saw the horse's spirit, though. And could this creature prance! There wasn't one ounce of casualness in this wonderful animal. I've ridden some horses where you had to touch their neck to see if they still had a pulse. But not this one.

I'm older now but not necessarily any wiser. I'd still rather ride one that kept me guessing what their next move would be than to plod along on to the barn. One article of pride that I always had was to never touch the saddle horn and to ride with my reins in one hand only. I'd rather go flying than be ashamed that I couldn't sit in the saddle without a crutch. Of course, today's drivers get around with only one hand on the wheel and with the new-fangled steering wheels you couldn't find the horn if you wanted to.

Backpacking

That time of year—when all I can do is make plans regarding future backpacking adventures, months in advance. The mountains where I travel in warmer seasons are inaccessible this time of year. Even in the summer months one must be careful of chosen routes that can become inaccessible due to weather. I don't know which is the toughest—backpacking up the mountain trails and over the boulders searching for new horizons, or the waiting part.

Years ago I would have placed my tent in a campsite with other families and shared a somewhat "social" existence. But I have found since that I don't leave society to return to its existence in more natural boundaries. When I go to the mountains it is to get away from what I left behind me. Backpacking allows me to do that for several reasons. To begin with, you can't take anything you can't carry with you. That does away with recreational vehicles, people walking through your camp site, alcohol parties until the early hours of the morning, generators starting up, people yakking when you're just about to doze off, smelly toilet facilities, flies and other pests in the camp ground locations, trash, and a host of other irritants. Not to mention there's nothing to see in the way of wildlife—just wild people who believe they're "roughing" it. But that's okay—I'd rather they stay where they are and allow me the chance to explore in solitude.

Sometimes I meet the occasional backpacker on a mountain trail and exchange cordial greetings and information about the path ahead. It's when I leave the trail and start my climb into the higher regions that I begin to finally breathe freedom. No more backpackers, horses or the casual fly fishermen heading for mountain trout. My prerequisites for a camp site when I finally decide to call it a day include a number of important details. First, I must be able to make it back out in case of bad weather. I try to choose a location that offers me an unobstructed view in all directions, and that provides breathtaking scenery. I want my shelter protected from the wind. And I want to feel the first rays of the morning sun when it crests the nearest mountain ridge for early morning warmth and dryness.

And privacy. I don't advertise my presence. I believe in the axiom of treading lightly and what you take in with you goes out with you in the way of trash. I drink water from the upper portions of fast-moving glacier waters that I treat accordingly. If I do heat any of my meals it is with a small camp fuel stove, which works great for coffee or hot cocoa too. I never take the dog with me because she makes too much noise and disturbs the wildlife, though she would be a good companion. I may take a good paperback book that I'm reading. I don't shave, but I do wash and brush my teeth away from any natural water source, and I take the necessary toilet articles and first aid items. I travel light, even if I feel like a pack horse with my gear. And I see sights that no postcard can depict. And I "feel" what I am living while in the mountains. If my son goes with me—all the better. I enjoy his company but know that the day will come when traveling with dad up some mountain trail may no longer be a main interest in life. And so, I will lose the companionship that I cherish in the high country—the ability to express with someone your feelings regarding the weather, scenery, wildlife and one's present thoughts. The social "being" in nearly everyone.

I know the dangers of climbing alone—and they are not limited to the elements or the wildlife. No, the real danger for me alone in the mountains is that, with no other person there with me, I have no obligation to get them back home safely. It's just me—and I am most dangerous to myself. With nothing to return for from the mountains, the day may arrive when I don't either...

Ponder

That time of year when we ponder. When is the next real holiday? The "seasonal" holidays are long gone. How long until spring arrives? How much do I owe the federal government in income taxes this year? And what have I been paying all of those taxes for throughout the previous year? More importantly, will the snow shovel hold together until the last snow falls? Will I ever be able to walk on solid ground again without ice under my feet, and the constant searching for anything to grab when the world goes up, and I go down? Should I wash the vehicle today in the hope that I'll get at least one day of driving around without it looking like it was built in the salvage yard? Will my energy bill exceed my total income this time around? I remember how the oil companies gouged me good back in the early 70's with their self-created shortages, and sold me their stockpiled fuel supplies at the increased rate.

Nothing has changed—just the years between then and now. Will California recover from its present dilemma of power outages? Ah hell, who cares about California anyway. If it's not earthquakes, mud slides, or brush fires then it's something else. Now I'll get back to more important items. Will I continue to get better looking as I advance in the years, or just turn into another AARP poster child?

I've never given any thought towards retirement. To me that's like figuring out what I want to do when I die. I've given some thought to chasing wild women, but at my age I have to be careful when I shovel the snow out of the driveway. My heart ain't a Timex—It my take a lickin' but it may not keep on tickin'. Of course, I've had some friends that aren't around anymore, having died at an earlier age than me. But I haven't got into reading the obituary page yet.

I keep telling myself that phrase—"The older the violin, the sweeter the music", but there's a lot of folks not listening to my type of music out there. Then, I consider what may be the next major event to enter into my life. Seems I've had enough "major events" already in my life and I can't imagine any other event sneaking up and surprising me. There's that other phrase too—"Been there, done that". But I still hold out hope that something great will come along that will knock me off my feet. (I just hope that it's not another new patch of ice.) No, I should say something "good", rather than "great". What's the difference between "good" and "great"? Now, I've something else to ponder!

Things

I don't have the ability to watch television because I don't have cable. But I don't miss it. I shoveled snow part of the day today because I don't have a snow blower. Since I've never had a snow blower I can't miss one.

I do get the local "Rag" delivered to the home every evening but only because I like to keep up with what's happening around the area. I don't get the newspaper for the news—it's too slanted with the editor's opinions. I don't have a good stylish winter coat that has all of the latest bells and whistles. But what I do have seems to keep me warm enough. Besides, I know that all of the latest technological fabrics melt when next to campfires, and snag easily. Same with gloves—they're all leather work gloves. I have three types of hats—baseball caps for around town, knit hats for extreme cold weather, and of course my cowboy hats for the hot days.

Growing up on the farm, our tractor never had an air conditioned/heated cab. Just a tractor seat for the heat, rain and cold. I don't have air conditioning in the house either. I don't have a dish washer—just my two hands and a sink. I don't have a trash compactor or a garbage disposal. I do keep my recycled items separate from the rest of the trash. I don't like watering the grass during the summer months because it seems like a waste of resources—not to mention that it would require more frequent cuttings with the lawnmower. I don't wear any jewelry.

I believe a good book will do you more good than a sleazy scandal sheet or a frilly magazine. I receive numerous advertisements on my email which I delete without reading. From time to time I get a phone call from someone trying to sell me something. I always tell them I'm not interested and when they go on to try and explain how whatever they are trying to sell me will be to my advantage I tell them "I'll bet you'll understand this…" and hang up on them.

I don't go to the bars and I am hesitant to attend any social events. I like my privacy. I don't "hit" on women and I believe that the man's role in this world is first to be a Gentleman. I think that the lowest form of life on this earth of ours is the man who strikes a woman. I would use that man for target practice. I don't tolerate rudeness from others. That's the surest way to get me into a confrontation.

I have "mellowed" some with age, but still have concern for my temper. I try to stay away from incidents that might make me regret my actions later on. I am a tough person to really know, but I have deep feelings and beliefs. I try not to make decisions for others and would rather they do those themselves.

I believe that the greatest gift a person can have in life is that of another person to share life with, and wish that were my present situation. I am constantly amazed at the number of folks who have lost touch with the world around them. I could occupy days just watching the clouds cast shadows across the land and visiting all the forms of wildlife. What my daughter and son think of their dad is more important to me than what others think of me.

For every wrong I've done to someone else, whether intentionally or not, I have felt lousy for it afterwards. Anytime someone says "Hi" and smiles at me they have unknowingly made that day the best in my life. It doesn't cost anything to be kind, but the rewards are great. So, the things that I don't have in my life, and that I don't miss, are far surpassed by the simpler things. And treasures they are. I firmly believe in human dignity and detest those who seek to remove the dignity of others. After all, I am happier with the things I have in my life, than the things I don't have.

Mountain Man

He had traveled here in the late summer of 1842. Known simply as a trapper, this was his second winter in the Shining Mountains. Much had been learned during these last seasons in the mountains, and his life had depended upon every lesson. He looked about his humble shelter. Spare traps hung from one wall along with the various dried meats, and roots from the summer season. Beaver pelts were stacked in one corner. Elk hides were stretched on another wall, as well as the one bear skin he was fortunate to have.

His bed, if one could call it that, was along another wall and consisted of a few blankets and hides. Fire light flickered shadows across this one room and illuminated briefly other accruements. His rifle lay within reach and leaned against the wall nearest to him. He had been lucky to have been able to purchase this fine percussion firearm in Saint Louis prior to his departure. His supplies were dwindling and he hoped that he would have sufficient quantities to see him through to the Rendezvous in June. He had enough black powder, lead and caps—that wasn't the problem. Salt and coffee supplies were getting low, as well as his tobacco supply.

This day had been a tough one. He had run his traps in the early morning and gathered only a few more beaver. This evening's check had produced nothing. And it was cold and getting colder. Snow had begun to fall again several hours ago but had ceased, as well as the wind. He didn't know what month it was or what time of the evening either. He kept track of time by the sun and the length of the daylight hours. The days were getting longer—must be either February or March, but he wasn't sure. He had been able to do some trading with the Crows a couple of months ago. That was the last time he had seen a human of any kind.

Placing another log on the fire, he watched as the sparks flitted past the opening of his shelter in this dark valley of snow and pine. Looking upward, it was clear this night, as he watched the heavens unfold into a canopy of stars. He heard his horse and mule nearby, restlessness in their movements, as they searched the snow for any morsel of food. The supply of bark he had gathered for them was in low supply and he knew he should be moving soon. This had been a good location for both shelter and trapping, but it was only temporary, as were the previous homes. His thoughts turned to the Spring Rendezvous. Months away, as well as any profit and supply that it might bring. He was still young but he knew that even the love of this wilderness and this life would one day come to an end. Wading in the cold streams and living this life among the ice and snow reminded him of that fact every day. If this weather held, then tomorrow would be a good time to pack up in search of a new place in these mountains.

He moved to the wall where his blankets and his hides were laid upon the ground and rolled himself up inside for warmth. The Rendezvous…Ah the Rendezvous. Warm times and company.

Angels

Angels amongst us. All shapes and sizes, personalities and differing characteristics. Long lost friends, those who shared their lives with ours in years past. For every conflict in our lives, an Angel stands beside us, watching. Each time we make a decision, take a course of action or reflect on past experiences, another Angel is watchful. Each hurt and each pain is endured by another Angel. Those times we feel so alone in our thoughts…are being shared by another. For every question asked, an answer is given. Unknown outcomes already known in advance by another who already knows how things will turn out in the end.

Angels are "personal"…that is, they are there right in front of us. Sometimes they look just like ordinary folks. They too, have their ups and downs. You would too if you knew what they already know. Sometimes we talk with Angels, without even knowing that we've done so. People become "conditioned" to their earthly existence, so much so that when presented with the real thing, they don't recognize what is before them. It's only after they have departed from our view, our lives, or our thoughts, that we realize just who we were visited by.

You can tell when you've been "visited" by an Angel. It's usually when things are so screwed up, that the peacefulness they drop on us from nowhere causes one to pause and think about what just happened. "Hey!…I was feeling lousy and now I feel great…What the heck?" Or, it's one of those times when for no apparent reason, a great, wonderful feeling comes over you. (You were just "touched" and are feeling the effect.) I've known a lot of Angels in my lifetime. I also know that's there's a lot more out there I haven't seen…yet. Another way you can tell when you've been "visited" by an Angel is that your life takes on a different focus—you see something that's been there all along but that you never looked at before. "Hey!…When did that get there?" Another hint that "someone" has just dropped in is when the person you're carrying on a conversation with looks at you like you're not there anymore. "Hey Buddy…you still with me?" "Ah, yea…I was just thinking…" Angels do some really strange things to us sometimes. Like when you catch yourself doing something, and wonder how you got there to begin with. You didn't have a slip of memory. No Sir! You were busy conversing with someone else and got so taken up in conversation that when you did finally come around you don't even remember how you got there.

There's a real comfort in associating with Angels. Kind of like a good night's sleep. If you're real sneaky…take a peek some night at the dark around you when you go to bed. See…all of that light. It was there all of the time. Angels amongst us.

The Boy

Once upon a time in a far away land…lived a boy with dreams as big as his heart. He lived on a farm beside a gently flowing stream amongst rolling hills and fields bordered by woods. In the spring the air would be filled with the fragrance from honeysuckle and lilac bushes. Locust trees grew straight upward to touch the sky. The farm yard was covered under the shade from three large Beech trees—one tree whose branches stretched outward as huge arms embracing all beneath. The grass upon which he walked barefoot was soft to the touch and provided comfort when he stretched out upon its carpet.

The nearest field was of alfalfa so thick and tall that its leafy stems reached past the boy's thighs. When he walked through the fields during the early morning hours the dew would drench his jeans and shoes. Butterflies fluttered around him as a cloud with their multitude of colors ranging in orange, white, black and yellow. This boy could venture to the stream and play as a sailor would upon the seas. Or he could walk the path to the furthest fields in search of new adventures.

Upon entering the woods the muskiness of the leafy vegetation and the shade would provide cooling comfort on a hot day. He would follow the game trails through the woods and into the open areas, down the ravines and back up to the crests of the hills. This boy love the Sycamore trees whose branches provided a natural ladder to the sky and he would build tree houses as high as the strongest limbs would allow. On a windy day he would climb the highest of these trees and in their uppermost branches sway with the wind as one would dance the waltz.

The boy could always find snakes, frogs, toads, turtles, groundhogs, deer and cottontails on his many excursions throughout the countryside. When the thunderstorms rolled in and the lightening cracked overhead he would wait with anticipation for the deep roar of thunder that was soon followed by the pelting raindrops. After the storm passed he could smell the freshness of its wrath. Leaves and small branches lay upon the damp ground. The dry earthen fields after these downpours would come alive with insects and earthworms. And everything was transformed into a darkened green resembling an African jungle. The sun would once more reappear and if the storm had passed just prior to sunset the ground would settle beneath the rising cloud of fog.

At night the crickets and locusts would harmonize the boy to sleep when he dreamily watched the fireflies dance above the fields. An owl would give its occasional voice to this natural orchestra of events while the stars brightened in the night skies. A gentle breeze would push the ground fog from the hills leaving behind the shadows of trees and bushes in its wake. The eastern sky would lighten with the Morning Dove's song softly awakening the boy from slumber. There was no urgency to be anywhere or to accomplish any task at this time of day…only to listen to the earth's heartbeat and the musical soul of its creatures.

Today's youth are pushed to sports, classes, work and other events. Their day begins with an alarm clock and the background noises of motorized traffic and the television or radio blaring out their advertisements and news stories. "Hurry up…you're late and don't forget…" Don't forget…that, once upon a time in a land far away…lived a boy with dreams as big as his heart, and a land to nourish those dreams.

Moving

I've been "mulling" over a few things lately. One of those things is where I want to live in about four months. This first of July I will have to be out of the home that I presently live in. Thomas will have graduated from high school by then—all the birds having left their nest. I've lived in Europe and in Asia and many locations throughout this great country of ours. I've endured the bitter cold in Korea along the DMZ and the desert heat as well. They say that "Home is where the heart is…" I know that there were a few places that were not "Home" because my heart sure wasn't there. But where I presently live has been a home for me these last ten years or so. I know that my heart has certainly been there most of the time.

So, in thinking about where I'd like to move to I of course have to consider things such as expenses and distance, for example. And of course, I would still enjoy the company and sanity of having my son with me as well. I think too that keeping my dog is important. Eleven years ago when she was just a pup I saved her from extermination scheduled for the following day, by adopting her. She's been by my side since then, so I owe it to her, as always. I'm not really an anti-social person, but enjoy my privacy. So, I think I would rather live out in the "boonies" somewhere when I do move. I'm an outdoor kind of feller—enjoying backpacking and hiking. But living in a tent the rest of my life leaves out some of the necessary comforts I've grown accustomed to.

I know that I'm getting older because the winters are felt more than before—but I'm not ready for heaven or hell, yet. I don't dislike the town I live in—I just want to live somewhere outside of town. It would be nice to be able to come home from a day's work and have running water as well. Of course, we didn't have water here again this last Friday and part of Saturday because the community I live in is too cheap to invest in the basic necessities for living. Somehow I just can't seem to rationalize the situation when it comes to laundry, taking a shower, washing dishes, toilet facilities or just having something to drink—and can't because there is no water available. But, that at least, will be behind me in four months.

No, I'd rather trust my own resources than to depend on others—even if they are paid for their lack of urgency or effort. So, in mulling where I'd like to live I've decided to let my heart choose instead. I've made rational choices before, to no avail. This time I say to hell with the brains side of it and let the heart take over instead. Of course…that may get me a pup tent on the sidewalk.

Statements

Some statements have always puzzled me. It doesn't take too much to puzzle me with some plain ordinary statements that I hear from time to time. But some stick in my mind just the same. Since I have always enjoyed traveling the back-country I am more "tuned" to particular statements regarding distances and locations, because they have a direct impact upon me and my travels.

For example—"You can't get there from here". Hummm. That makes me think about where I should be in order to get there. If it's not "here" where am I supposed to be, then where is it I should be to get there? It sounds to me as if it's a lost cause. Obviously I'm not in the right location to begin my journey to that destination, but why can't I get there from here? I've been to a lot of places I should not have been. I got there somehow. Where do I go to start all over?

Another statement has always puzzled me—"It's not in the middle of nowhere, but you can see it from there". Now that one really makes me think. I'd have to work really hard to get to nowhere, just to see what it is I'm looking for. I think I've been in a few places that were "nowhere", but I'm not sure. I've met an occasional stranger in the middle of nowhere—and wondered how they got there. They might have thought that they couldn't get there from here, but they did get there, as well as I got there—"nowhere".

Then there's that statement regarding distance—"It's twenty miles as the crow flies". When someone tells me that regarding the distance I must still travel I know that I'm in serious trouble, for two reasons. To begin with, I believe they are referring to straight-line distance. If they're talking about that distance and I'm in the mountains, then I know to at least double the distance. The other part "as the crow flies" really puts a damper on things as well. I've never seen a crow fly any further than from tree to tree—certainly not twenty miles between trees, and never upon a straight flight course. So I have to infer that besides the supposed straight-line distance, I'm going to have to travel ziz-zag from place to place and up and down the terrain features as well.

You can imagine how disheartening that can be on an individual. What starts as a simple backpacking excursion in the mountains becomes a major disaster—just by asking the simple question of where something is located and how far it is to get there. Question: "Do you know where Cloud Peak is?" Answer: "Yea—I know where it is, but you can't get there from here! It's not in the middle of nowhere, but you can see it from there. Actually, it's about twenty miles from here—as the crow flies!" That's when all of my thought processes just jell up and I get that far-away look in my eyes. Then, I remember two simple statements that overcome everything—"Make it happen!" That's how you get to the top of the mountain. And, "Just do it!"

Cowboy

The wind blows gently through the prairie grasses as the sun begins its slow decent behind the hills to the west. I can barely see the outline of the distant mountains—still slightly snow-capped, and over a hundred miles away. Hues of blue sculptures floating on the horizon. My horse snorts and the leather creaks as I turn in the stirrups to watch the dusk rise upward. My right arm upon the saddle horn, reigns loosely held in my left hand as I cross my left arm over my right, and give my horse slack to lower his head and browse.

Far off, I hear the restless sound of coyotes as they begin their nocturnal journey. The landscape to the east now grows darker and the early moon breaks above the rolling hills. Pockets of warm air on the high ground contrast with the cooler air in the shallow valleys I have just traveled through. A jackrabbit skips around the sage in search of an evening snack. I hear my horse as he pulls the grass from the soil—pawing for new territory and fresher stems.

It never ceases to amaze me how the land transforms itself from dawn until dusk. There is greater clarity in the still morning air, before the sun begins to warm up the atmosphere and distort the far-away images. By late morning, the waving patterns of heat drifts upward and the ever so slight haze makes clarity of sight difficult. In the middle of the afternoon, the temperature climbs and working in the sun becomes a task. But this platter of earth finally tilts in the late afternoon and the shadows lengthen. It finally begins to cool again. The evening meal is always the most enjoyable—the day's work is done and trading stories with the other hands while enjoying a cup of coffee over the dinner table loosens the spirits and eases one's muscles.

There's no need to saddle up afterwards but I do because, while enjoy the companionship of talk; I need my horse to take me to where I can privately reflect upon my own thoughts. And so begins the short journey to my favorite hilltop where I watch the world to my right grow darker, and the world to my left gather the last remaining rays of light before turning to a final glow. Solitude and peacefulness, and a chill in the early evening air.

The sweet scent of sage carried on the breeze gradually fades as I gently pull my horse's head up and turn him once more towards the ranch buildings far away. I am eighteen and I have a full life ahead of me. In a few days I'll be taking the bus back to the Midwest once more. I don't know if or when I'll ever be this way again, so the pictures I place carefully in my mind's scrapbook are most important to me. At least in my heart I'll always remain…a cowboy.

Bull Weather

Spring has arrived in Wyoming—I know, because the weather never stays the same from one day to the next. No need to worry or complain about "the same 'ol weather"—not around here anyway. This time of year is unpredictable. Never know what is going to happen next. "Weather" is just one of those things that you can't count on. One day it's in the 60's and that night there's a blizzard.

Couple of weeks ago Thomas was leaving the high school when some kid plowed into the back of his truck. Took out the rear bumper and dented in the corner of the quarter panel on Thomas' truck. The cost amounted to seven-hundred and eighty-two bucks worth of damage in a school parking lot. I picked-up a new bumper for the truck today that I had ordered but I have to wait until it's warmer (above freezing at night) to do the body work. So, who knows when that will be, what with the spring weather.

Then there's that time change thing again this weekend. "Spring forward." I wish that I could "spring", but I can't, anymore. Not sure if I ever could "spring" or not. I've "sprung" a few things in my life though.

This weekend is the Bull Wars rodeo at the Camplex. Now there's a golden opportunity to watch a cowboy get hammered without having a drink in his hand. I took lunch alongside the road in Rozet today while the snow was flying horizontal. Off in the field behind the Rozet post office I watched several long-horns graze. Got to thinking that I haven't seen a rodeo yet where any cowboy rode a longhorn for eight seconds for the thrill and excitement of it all. Haven't seen any longhorns in a rodeo, come to think of it.

Some folks would let you believe that bulls are like the Wyoming weather—unpredictable. But I don't buy into that. Bulls are nasty all of the time. I've known a lot of "Cowpunchers" in my time but no "Bullpunchers". Funny, how the word "Bull" gets wrapped into so many adjectives. Like—"Bull Market". (Haven't seen one of those either.) Or, "Bull Whip". (Use a whip on a bull and he'll take it away from you!) I'm not sure what "Bull Headed" has to do with some folks. Can't figure out if it means they're stubborn, have a big head, or if they're horny.

At any rate, I'll probably go to the rodeo to see if any "Cowpunchers" can ride for eight seconds. In the meantime, I'll just deal with the spring weather, set my clocks forward if they're not "sprung", and slap the new bumper on Thomas' truck. The only predictable thing I know for sure is that I'm full of "Bull...."

Water Leak

One of those days today. Funny how things start slow then go into self-destruction. It started with a one o'clock appointment for a reverse osmosis routine maintenance at a customer's location. The maintenance part went okay—it was what happened next that sent things into anything but "routine". Normally, I can do this particular service in less than an hour-and-a-half. Conduct all of the required test procedures, change the filters, re-pressure and disinfect the storage tank and system etc. Turn the water pressure back on and check for water leaks.

Yikes! A drip of water coming from a compression fitting that I haven't touched. I explain to the customer that they have a leak. "Well, can you fix it?" My answer of course is, "I'll do my best." I take the plumbing apart and reinstall the water line. It still leaks—and now I have another leak from beneath the water faucet fixture as well. (I haven't touched that one either!) I explain to the customer "Well, there's more than one leak here." Their response is of course, "Well, it wasn't leaking before you got here!" My answer of course is, "Well, it sure is now!" They ask, "Are you a plumber?" My answer is of course is, "No! Did you folks install this or someone else?" Their answer, "We had a plumber install this less than a year ago and it's still under warranty." I say (to me of course) "You should have had another plumber do this job because this is all screwed-up!"

I call the boss and explain the situation. "Well, do they think we're the cause of their leak?" My answer of course is, "Sure, they think we're the cause of their leak, because I'm here now working on their reverse osmosis and their plumbing wasn't leaking before I got here!" The boss says to do what I need to get it repaired. The customer asks if I know of any good plumbers and that they were not going to call the guy that installed this system, warranty or not! Well, since the faucet and water lines are under warranty I decide to do the job myself.

Of course, I can't remove the faucet from the stainless steel sink because there is no work area to get my tools into. The customer goes back into their office and I tear into the project. I remove the water lines, the drain lines and all of the other items necessary—then I remove the sink itself. I take the entire sink with me back into town to the location where everything was purchased by the customer. Needless to say—they don't have an exact faucet in stock. But, working with the customer and the supply house we agree on an exchange of materials. The customer comes out ahead in the deal for costs, and a better faucet and plumbing system.

I drive all the way back out of town and upon arrival; I reinstall the sink and all of the plumbing fixtures. No leaks. The reverse osmosis is working well. The water is on and the customer likes the newer system better than what they had. And I am…out of there! I do my own electrical work, my own automotive work, and my own plumbing work as well. I do all of my computer hardware and software work also. So there is nothing more frustrating to me than when something that belongs to someone else breaks, and they look at you as if you were the cause. All of us have the knack of being at the wrong place at the wrong time sometimes. I'm not an electrician, mechanic, plumber or computer wizard. But I can't afford not to be either.

Diabetes

I've known some folks who died years ago, and are still walking around. "Something" came into their life and took that life from them. They may not have noticed their life's absence, but other people sure have noticed it. They're not the same person they were at one time.

I enjoy looking at photographs—especially those taken years ago. Photos are a time capsule. Sure, they meant something of interest when taken at the time. But their real meaning is more prevalent years later as time passes. The picture is placed in a shoe box, a closet, or just forgotten until one finds it. "Ah yes, I remember now what it was I was doing when that photo was taken." I remember the year, the events current at the time, what was going on in my life then, and how I felt. A time capsule in a photograph.

We don't always have that same insight when we consider past events that changed our lives. We just change in some way unrecognizable to ourselves, but noticed by others. Some people we know are a real blessing in our life because they have encountered life-changing events in their lives and continue to live their life unburdened. My daughter is like that. Several years ago when she called me from the intensive care unit in Denver and told me that she was diagnosed with Type I diabetes I was a wreck. I was crushed. I asked myself a thousand times "Why her? Why not me? Anyone, but not my daughter!" But she is an absolute example of living life in a positive manner and never giving up.

And so, I'll never give up in helping find a cure for diabetes for her and the other sixteen million. As long as I live—I will continue to strive towards overcoming this terrible disease and finding a cure. We all die eventually—some sooner than others. Blame it on heredity, genes, lifestyle or whatever. But not everyone lives life as it was meant to be lived. That should not be a deterrent keeping us from striving though. The easy choice is to give up, not to think about it, or run from the fear of it all. But, every little bit of effort that we exert towards overcoming obstacles in our lives brings us that much more closely to life itself.

We are all destined to die, but no one individual is destined to live, unless they personally make that choice. I know some who are scared to death of commitment, or of making a decision because they worry what others may think of them. They live their own life in the shadow of others—never becoming the individual they were destined to become. True feelings of fear are much like a time when one is confronted with a life-threatening situation and their response is to scream in anguish at what threatens them. The heart beats faster, the eyes become focused, the mind becomes sharpened, and muscles flex—and one strikes back at the threat to one's life. It's only when we don't realize that what confronts us as a threat and we don't react, and instead accept it, that it destroys us.

When I eventually find a cure for diabetes—then I'm going to go to work on a new fear. In the meantime I will continue to scream in anguish, fight in every manner I can invent, and admire the past and present photos of living examples.

April 22, 1805

Excerpt from the Journal of Meriwether Lewis dated April 22, 1805:

"walking on shore this evening I met with a buffaloe calf which attached itself to me and continued to follow close at my heels untill I embarked and left it. it appeared allarmed at my dog which was probably the cause of it's so readily attatching itself to me."

With hopes, fears, ambitions and tears, wearing first a smile then a frown, experiencing personal ups and downs, while maintaining a steady course along crooked trails, to reach the summit and then to plummet, and to begin anew what was begun. So it was for those who walked a path in the wild and balanced their existence on life's edge. To have been the few who were the first to have viewed this land, before the pioneer's arrival, and to have enjoyed its natural unspoiled beauty as God intended it to be, would have gained the greatest treasure of all.

Before domestic livestock and agriculture, exploitation of mineral and fuel, homes and families, highways and cities, fences and transmission lines, dams and power plants, noise and pollution, there existed the wind upon the prairie grasses and in the mountain passes, and a songbird's melody. No cars, trucks, trains or planes. Just the wind carrying the song of life to those still capable of hearing the music.

We gained material wealth in the years that followed, but have lost our souls in doing so. And in giving our souls in exchange for material wealth, we have destroyed not only the land, but ourselves in the process. So it was for those who walked a path in the wild and balanced their existence on life's edge. What was shall never be again.

Thomas' Truck

This one is for the guys out there. I look forward to the weekends as a chance to relax and take leisure seriously. So, I'm sitting at the 'ol computer Saturday evening when Thomas comes into the house and says "Dad!" Now, I know that my weekend is about to change when my son expresses himself like that. "What's up?" I ask. "Dad, my truck won't start and it's on the road over by Church and Stanley." (He had just skateboarded home out of breath to let me know.) So, off we went in my truck to see if we could get his truck going.

Now, a spring storm is brewing at this time—the winds are gusting and the dust is flying, and the clouds are getting dark, and the area where his truck is located is well…not an area you would leave anything valuable overnight if you wanted to find it the next day. So we get there and sure enough, the starter spins but the engine won't crank. I don't have a receiver hitch on my truck yet (my next project) so I can't tow him back home about a quarter mile away, and I don't dare leave it where it is. So I have him get into the driver's seat to steer and I push the truck on my own two feet back home. Then, we turn around and walk back to get my truck still parked where his was located previously.

Now it's starting to rain and the wind is blowing sand and scoria in our eyes, but we finally make it to my truck and drive it back home. I tell him it's too late now to do anything because the auto stores are closed and the only place open is Checker Auto on Sunday. Of course, he needs his truck for work and school. This Sunday morning I go out at six-thirty and remove the starter from his truck and at nine o'clock I'm there at Checker to have the starter bench-tested. It works okay. So I go back home, thinking that perhaps there's a bad electrical connection on his truck—reinstall the old starter, clean and check all of the electrical cables and…the same thing. So I'm thinking the old starter can't handle the load against the ring gear, take it back to Checker Auto and buy a new starter. I reinstall the new starter—and it spins but won't crank the engine. Now, I know I've got some serious trouble internally with the engine. So I take apart the distributor cap, put my socket and ratchet on the crank and turn the engine over by hand. The rotor in the distributor does not turn. Next, I remove everything on the front of the engine down to the block and sure enough, the timing belt is destroyed. Wonderful! So I take the two timing belts to Checker Auto (after Thomas had called them with the information I provided him about his truck) to get the new timing belts, because they said that they had both belts. Well, they only had one belt (the one that wasn't broken—yet) and I found out that it wasn't the right one either.

Now that I have his engine disassembled—I still don't have the parts. Next, I call a friend to see about opening up NAPA for me. We meet over at the store, but he doesn't have the belt either—so I order it from Billings, Montana and it should be here in two days. Meanwhile, "back at the ranch", I still don't know if the truck has any serious engine damage from the timing belt breakage. It is possible that the pistons may have slammed into the valves when the belt gave out. I won't know that until Tuesday evening if and when the ordered timing belt arrives, and I get everything reassembled with the engine timed again. No—I didn't return the new starter because the old starter was dry in the bearings and would probably go next. But I did return the one wrong timing belt back to Checker Auto, and they do stock the receiver hitch for my truck, when that project comes around.

Let's see now…what have I accomplished this weekend so far? I removed Thomas' truck from a "war-zone" area and nearly had a cardiac doing so. I've visited Checker Auto four times in one day. I bothered some good NAPA folks. Smeared grease on my arms and face for good measure. Got a truck in pieces and no parts. Over $150.00 in the hole and nothing to show for it so far. And I don't even know if the engine is "toast" yet. When your son comes in the house out of breath and says "Dad!"…it's time to hide.

Individuals

What a day to make one reflect about things! I'll explain, and hope that you'll have the patience and understanding to follow along with my present thought processes. Let me begin by saying that I was out of town for most of the day, so none of the individuals I refer to live in the Gillette, Wyoming area. Let's just say that there are four "types" of people that I encountered today—either directly or indirectly, and I'll just "label" them "A", "B", "C", and "D".

To start with, individual "A" is a older person and lives alone. This individual is very kind and considerate and is appreciative that I am there. Everything this individual owns is right before one's eyes. The home is old and worn and out in the countryside. It's been there for many years, as has this individual and the family. The photographs that adorn the home are mostly old pictures of years gone by, and are mostly of other members of the family. The pictures tell the history of this individual and the family—from childhood to old age. The photos also show who is no longer there anymore.

Individual "B" also owns a home in the countryside. It is more modern, nicely furnished and recently remodeled. Individual "B" has worked hard throughout life as well. This individual is not nearly as old as individual "A", but is just as considerate and appreciative of my presence. The home has quality in appearance and affluence as well. There are family photos of more recent times, even though the previous family members no longer live with this individual and have homes of their own in other places now. I am just as comfortable here as I was with individual "A", though the home lacks the "live-in" look. (In other words—one should check the bottom of one's boots before walking across the carpet.) This individual is much more talkative—enjoys a good conversation and asks many questions.

Individual "C" is not home when I arrive, but I have this individual's permission to enter the premises while nobody is there. I haven't seen individual "C" in almost a year now—nor have I talked with this person for that length of time. I have no idea when individual "C" will return—because this person only lives out here in the countryside for a few months during the summer. The rest of the time this individual is elsewhere in the world. The "home" is extravagant and immense, as are all of the outlying buildings and the other "homes" for guests that visit this individual. Yes, individual "C" is very wealthy, but is considerate. And if this individual was at home, would be appreciative that I was there. The photographs that are everywhere depict power and prestige with other important people. The art and sculpture are from around the world. There are more bathrooms, kitchens, living rooms, offices and bedrooms than what I can remember counting, in this one house alone. Let's just say that there isn't a home in all of Gillette, Wyoming that even comes close to the millions of dollars spent on individual "C's" house and guest houses.

I see individual "D" walking along Interstate 90 as I am driving back towards town. This person is carrying a backpack and sleeping bag on the back. This person is "hitchhiking"—which is legal in Wyoming, but does not display the "thumb" and so I assume this person has accepted the fact that if a ride is to be had, then someone will stop. Otherwise, individual "D" continues to walk along the interstate with everything owned on the backside and accepts whatever fate encountered. I don't know if this person has a home or family, or a defined direction of travel. As a matter of fact—I know less about this individual that any of the previous people on today's journey.

So, you may ask—"Where am I going with this?" To begin with, none of the individuals have exhibited any "predispositions" towards me. They have accepted me as I am—as I have done towards them. Contrast this with other people that I have contact with on a daily basis who know that they are better than me, have been more fortunate in life than I have been, and are neither considerate nor appreciative when I arrive at their home. They are demanding, sometimes rude and indifferent, and let you know right away that you do not "fit-in" their life at all. Their "self-centered character" shines like a strobe light in the darkness. I am polite and courteous—and silently laugh at their menial thoughts towards me.

How little they really know, and how shadowed they are by the likes of individuals "A", "B", "C", and "D". If only they and so many other individuals like themselves, would allow the smallest pretense of humanity and humility to rise to the surface, what a better world this would be.

May 5, 1864

In many parts of our country this time of year, we celebrate the welcomed warmth of spring and the beginnings of new life. It should be remembered that this was not how some of our great ancestors remembered these particular days of May 5th and May 6th. For on this day in 1864 a great battle was taking place. "Eastern Theater, Battle Of The Wilderness—Federal General Warren notifies Grant and Meade of an enemy force—Ewell's—on the Orange Turnpike; thinking that this is only a division, Grant orders Warren to attack.

These forces quickly join in a fierce battle, and it becomes clear that Lee's army is opposing the Federals in force. Because of the thick woods, the men often grapple at almost point blank range; battle lines become confused in the smoke-filled forest, regiments losing contact with one another. Soldiers and leaders follow the battle by the sound of firing, and often find themselves shooting at an enemy they can only see by the flashing of guns. Late in the afternoon Confederate General Hill's advance along the Plank Road is met by Hancock; a separate and equally desperate contest ensues. Again the fighting is at close quarters, often hand-to-hand with bayonets and clubbed muskets, the artillery silent for fear of doing harm to unseen friendly troops. All day the fighting surges back and forth, but as evening falls nothing significant has been gained by both side, and the forces retire to await the next day's battle.

During the night, troops of both sides frequently wander into enemy lines...During the night Grant orders a general attack by Sedwick, Warren, and Hancock, to commence at 5 o'clock in the morning. Reinforcements are moved up on both sides. Before the Union advance can be launched, however, Rebels attack Sedwick on the Union right flank, and the firing gradually spreads along the line. Federal General Hancock moves against the weak positions of Hill, who has unwisely failed to entrench his forces. Hill's lines are soon enveloped on the Orange Plank Road and are in danger of being routed. But at the critical moment, Longstreet's reinforcements, awaited by Hill since the previous day, make a dramatic appearance, moving down the Orange Plank Road at a trot. Soon the Union advance is checked and the Federals thrown back to their original breastworks; a further Confederate advance captures these works, but is not able to break the Union line.

About 10 o'clock in the morning, after turning back the Union advance, Longstreet decides to take the offensive against the Federal left flank. He finds an unfinished railroad cut that provides a clear route to the Federal flank and sends four brigades to the attack. Before noon the Federals are overwhelmed by theses forces; the Union left is rolled up northward in confusion. But then disaster strikes the Confederate advance, as recounted by Southern General E M Law: 'General Longstreet rode forward and prepared to press his advantage...Longstreet and Kershaw rode with General Jenkins at the head of his brigade as it pressed forward, when suddenly the quiet that had reigned for some moments was broken by a few scattered shots on the north of the road, which were answered by a volley from Mahone's line on the south side. The firing in their front, and the appearance of troops on the road whom they failed to recognize as friends through the intervening timber, had drawn a single volley, which lost to them all the fruits of the splendid work they had just done. General Jenkins was killed and Longstreet seriously wounded by our own men.' As he is taken from the battlefield, Longstreet orders General Field to press the attack, but the Confederate forces are in confusion after the accident; Lee comes forward to organize the forces, but the impetus has been lost and the Federals have time to regroup and fortify their positions.

A Confederate attack later in the afternoon is halted at the Union breastworks...Causalities in the two days of fighting have been staggering: the North has lost 2246 killed, 12,037 wounded, and 3383 missing, a total of 17,666 of 100,000 engaged; the Confederate losses, from the usual incomplete records kept on southern causalities, are something over 7500 of 60,000 engaged; the Union losses are thus more than twice the Confederate, but the North has lost only a slightly larger percentage of its army than has the South. Although the troops do not yet know it as they entrench in the evening, the Battle of the Wilderness is over.

But the tragedy is not quite over as darkness falls. Brush fires have broken out in the thick woods; several times during the day the fighting has stopped by mutual consent while soldiers of both armies move their wounded out of the burning woods. During the night the forest fires rage, and while the entrenched armies listen to the screams of the trapped, 200 Federal wounded die in the flames…"

Touch a flower, smell the sweetness in the air, and hear the music of a song-bird's melody. And remember, that it wasn't always so in May of 1864.

Going Home

There's a particular loneliness when one views the far horizon from a prominent height. Even when on the prairie, the distance forces you to focus on the faintness of vistas seen. Only in the West, can one become totally immersed with the unbelievable landscape. This land captured my heart as a young man, and its views will always remain there—locked away in my memory.

I have been so fortunate in my lifetime to have experienced these sights and to have taken breath of the life it provided. The people that inhabit this western region are unique, personal, and have the necessary stamina to survive this sometimes harsh and rigorous environment. I was a cowboy in Wyoming in 1968, visited the Wyoming regions again in 1984, and made it my home in 1989. Much has changed in those years—and for me personally, the last several years have taken so many different paths.

A few days ago I decided to follow a different trail. Much like my own trail through life, the mountains and the prairies have provided me with insight that few have had the opportunity to follow. So, I will be leaving Wyoming June 2nd and moving back to Indiana. I hope to settle down in either the Martinsville or Indianapolis area, and I will be staying for awhile on the farm where I grew up as a boy, until I get things going the right direction once more. My daughter, Amanda will remain in Denver. My son, Thomas has thus far indicated that he will remain in Gillette while he works towards more definite future plans. It was sixteen years before I was able to travel alone, to the West once more. And it will be sixteen years that I will travel alone to the East again. Only this time, Tippy will accompany her Master on his journey.

I have stood upon the Oregon Trail, knelt and felt with my fingers the wagon wheel ruts left in the rock by those early pioneers. I have felt what they must have felt, in seeking a new life in a different land so far from home. It was the "destination" uppermost in their minds that caused them to seek out a new life for themselves. I did not feel the need of destination so much as I felt their journey. And so, it is not the "destination" but the journey that I seek…and the trail of life that continues onward. Once more, I look to new horizons.

Rat Race

Ice tea weather—in the 90's these last several days here in Wyoming. And no matter what, "Human Nature" has not yet forced us to complain about it being so hot. The "cold" days are too recent in memory, and it's supposed to cool down again this week. A busy weekend is over. Worked on Thomas' truck—which seems to have a bad ignition switch harness that I'll have to replace. But, that is good news (except for the cost) because Thomas and I had a good conversation on Saturday evening about his staying here in Wyoming. A father to son talk (unlike a boss to employee talk) yielded more positive results with him reaching the decision that going back to Indiana with his 'ol man is okay.

So, when I replace the ignition switch harness it will be a reward for me. I also installed a radio in his truck and one in mine—so we'll be able to communicate to each other from two different vehicles on the way back. My cell phone will also be upgraded before I leave, to "digital"—since the Indianapolis area is digital now and not analog. So, if need be, I will be able to send and receive phone calls on the way back anywhere in the United States without long-distance or roaming charges, and the phone will be internet ready (no laptop computer required).

I have a big portable kennel for the dog which will go into the bed of my truck. When I'm tired of driving I'm getting into the kennel and Tippy can take over for me. She's a good dog…but a lousy driver. (She looks goofy in sunglasses too.) If only I can get into "warp speed" on the way back to cut down on travel time. I haven't started packing yet, but the empty boxes are showing up for future use. I'm going to wait until the last minute to pack, and then drink a case of beer to get ready. When I'm snookered I'll call it quits and go with a light load. (One of those "Here…hold my beer and watch this…" Wyoming driver moves.) Pulling a trailer over 1,239 miles won't be much joy. I don't plan to stop for any motels—just gas, food and stretching three pairs of legs. When we get tired we'll just pull over and sleep for awhile.

Either way, it's still about twenty-four hours of straight driving to get to the farm. Once we cross the Missouri River we'll be back in the Midwest. Once we cross the Mississippi River we'll be back East. (That's "Western" terminology for "Easterners".) I'm not sure if we'll travel through any "civilized" country though. Seems that we'll be leaving "civilization" behind in Wyoming. I've been gone so long now that I don't know what they call "civilization" back home in Indiana. "Rat Race" sounds familiar.

Energy

Where do we go, when there are no new unexplored horizons? This Mother of ours—Earth, is our only home in all of the celestial creation. I've often wondered if there yet still exists a place than someone has not yet traveled or looked upon here on this planet of ours. Certainty in the populated areas of our great cities and suburbs not one inch of land has remained untouched by mankind. But what of the great expanse in the remote regions of our great nation?

It seems to me that, the more interstate highways and roads that traverse this land, the less traveled unpaved areas become. The nature of mankind is to build and to make life easier. Our great technology in the extraction of minerals and fuels is designed to provide us with all the necessary comforts of life. The production of energy keeps us fueled in the way of electricity, lighting, heating, and air conditioning—and creates the "home" environment where we can sleep, eat and just participate in our recreational activities. It also provides our work environment and most of our social environment. We tend to think of ourselves as intelligent creatures capable of producing all forms of energy.

Our dependence upon energy has become so paramount in importance that it surpasses the existence of our basic needs to exist. We give little regard to the origin of our water supply, the food that we eat or the materials required in the clothing we wear or the homes we build. But, if we should lose even for a short duration the electricity that provides us with so many of the necessary comforts in our lives—we are in turmoil. No heat, air conditioning, lights, phones, microwaves, washers and dryers. No stoves to cook our meals, to pump our water or to heat it. No television, newspaper or computer. No fuel from the gas pumps, or directional signals at intersections. No music to listen to. No light in the darkness to read a book or magazine. No radar for the aircraft overhead. No radios or communication. No business can operate. All comes crashing to a halt—nothing works. We produce for ourselves the essentials required for our very exist-ence—to include electricity.

The one thing that we do not create—is energy. In all of our "civilized" societ-ies, not once have we produced energy. We have "used" more energy in the extraction process than we have "created". The minerals and fuels that provide us with the comforts and necessities in our lives are not renewable. Once they are used—they are gone and will never be replaced again. Only in Mother Nature is "life" found to be self-sufficient and renewable. All that is used in living—is replaced again through the "circle-of-life" process. Mankind is not presently capable of this process because his intent has always been to "use" and not to "renew". We "extract" but never "replace". We live for "today", and not "tomor-row". That is why fuel prices continue to climb and why there are power outages. As long as we "demand", the "supply" will surely follow. The costs are paid by each and every one of us—now, and into the future.

Our Mother cannot provide for us if we do not nurture her and love her. No one person can stand alone and live life separate from our society today. And yet, our civilization's total existence is dependent entirely upon this Earth of ours. Our only home that we continue to "trash" on a daily basis. If we do not climb out of our present mentality and pursue other alternatives to supply our energy needs other than those we currently utilize—then we will give ourselves to extinc-tion.

Leaving Wyoming

So many memories. Arriving in Wyoming for the third time in my life—first in 1968, then 1984 and finally in 1989. This has been my longest stay in the High Plains region. The wind can be a blessing and fixes oneself to the land and sky. It bridges the distance. While some may complain—it has filled my sails on this River Of Life. The stars have illuminated the heavens and the moon has touched my soul. The waters have run cold and clear in my veins. The prairie has com-forted me and the mountains have lifted my spirits. I have walked the glaciers and the grasses. The pines have whispered me to sleep at night. The Meadowlark has been my wake-up call in the morning.

This will be my last "Considerations" from Wyoming. Future writings will come from home in Indiana where I hope to acquire the inspiration and insight of that region once more. I'm a bit older than eighteen now but my perception of life has not dimmed throughout the years. One of the hardest things for me is to say goodbye to those who have been a part of my life. I'm not any good at farewells—I do better in greeting folks I guess. There are a lot of good people here who have provided me with a book of knowledge. The saying goes that a friend is one who knows everything about you, and likes you anyway. I plan to reopen my web site once I get situated and I find an internet provider back in Indiana. Of course the "theme" won't be western anymore, but it will still have some of the pages dedicated to events and individuals that I had in the last web site. And I will continue to pester you with emails and other trivia because I am a firm believer that "out of sight" shouldn't necessarily mean "out of mind".

It will be good to be with family again and hopefully I won't wear out my welcome too soon. If I had to pen a description of myself for posterity, I would not have to think too hard about how I would want others to think of me. Simply—I would want to be remembered as a "good 'ol boy". That would be the final gift that I could wish for at the completion of this time on earth. In 1968 I attended the Cheyenne Frontier Days for the first time in my life. I saw the West in all of her glory. Cheyenne was "the" town—still kind of rough and tumble. Lot of old timers were still around then who were born in the late 1800's and they could spin quite a few good yarns for this youngster of a cowboy. And I cherished their stories and the portraits of their lives.

So as I prepare once more to depart this grand and wonderful West, I'll just say goodbye the way they would have done:

> *My foot's in the stirrup,*
> *My pony won't stand;*
> *Goodbye, old partner,*
> *I'm leaving Cheyenne.*

Part Two: Back to the Midwest

Tippy's Death

This afternoon I shoveled the last of the soil over the grave of my beloved dog, Tippy. I laid the logs above the mound and later placed a cross with her collar hung from the cross, and silently said my last farewell to my dog.

Tippy was hit on the road sometime early this morning. My son and I were not there because we had just moved to our apartment at Greenwood, Indiana the day before and we are still unpacking from the move. I think that some day in the far future we may be fortunate enough to finally feel at home somewhere, and perhaps this will be the place.

So much to do, and so many things have happened in our lives in the journey from Wyoming. I would like to think that Indiana could be our home, but I'm not sure of anything presently. I've had too much turmoil and upheaval these last two months and the faith I brought with me from the West is dwindling fast.

I know that home is where the heart is…and I am still in search of that home. I think of the trip eastward and how the world changes with distance. I miss the mountains and the prairie. I am not fond of the humidity and lack of a good cool breeze. But I grew up in these parts—and today I wonder if I will ever grow up again. I feel a deep loss of freedom and satisfaction in who I am and especially when I can do so little for others. But we are in our new home now, and still planning to make a life here.

Donna said that Tippy just stood in the road yesterday and watched us leave in the moving truck. Last night Tippy wouldn't eat anything after she couldn't go with us. I guess she was free for the first time in her life. But she was not home.

Air Conditioning

Before air conditioning in homes I guess we sweated. We did have electric fans though, to circulate the humid air. This home of ours has central air. Without it I guess I would melt. Back in Wyoming the swamp cooler did the trick to keep one cool. If you used a swamp cooler in these parts you could go swimming in sweat.

Air conditioning helps one sleep. It also muffles a lot of the outside noise with all of the doors and windows closed. Here in Greenwood the outside noise is not necessarily that of nature either. When I go outside at four-thirty in the morning prior to going to work I get to feel the first indication of the left-over night air. But I also get to hear the morning birds as well. There's a Dove or two in the area that I listen to prior to dawn. And of course there are the Robins.

Grandmother once told me that when she was a child that she had neighbors whose last name was "Geese". One day when that particular lady of that household was outside by herself my Grandmother said good morning to her using proper English and called her "Mrs. Goose" (the singular form of Geese). I'm not sure how that went over with Mrs. Geese.

Neighbors being what they are—I have still not met any of ours here in this new location. Everyone keeps to themselves mostly and I would feel odd knocking on someone's door and introducing myself as their next door neighbor. I could imagine the thoughts racing through their minds as they peer through the peep-hole and see this old fart smiling back at them. They would probably say to they're live-in girlfriend, "Hey Babe, there's a lunatic outside our door smiling through the peep-hole at me".

Times have changed I guess. In Grandmother's time there weren't any live-in girlfriends, or peep-holes. Folks didn't lock their doors either. And homemade "Justice" took care of the lunatics. Indiana has changed from the farm country than I knew as a boy to the metropolitan theme of today. And the more people there are, the fewer the interactions. Air conditioning has helped this process along, whether at home or in your auto, the "outside" world is kept away. As for myself, I enjoy the touch of reality once in awhile. So what if it's hotter than a firecracker and I have the truck windows rolled down when I'm driving down a country road. A good breeze and an occasional insect that zips through my side window doing sixty mph keeps one alert. And even though I do have central air conditioning I am still sleeping on the floor at night because I really balk at spending so much money on a bed that I'll only sleep in on an average of five hours a night.

I know that if you're really tired you can sleep anywhere. Horses are good example of that. I tried sleeping standing up but that just doesn't work for me. And I tried sleeping without air conditioning here in this humid weather, and that doesn't work. But for me, all of that is just to get me to the point where at four-thirty in the morning I can go outside and listen to the morning birds. They don't have air conditioning either.

Hooters

Tonight, Thomas and I went to eat supper at Hooters here in Greenwood. I had never been to Hooters before. (Thomas said he had eaten at Hooters once at Fort Collins, Colorado.) I read about the history of Hooters printed on the back of their menu. I'm still trying to figure out where the "owl" part fits in the history of things.

Anyway, late yesterday afternoon there was knock on our door, which I opened to find a young black gentleman trying to sell some cleaning compounds, door to door. I explained that we had just moved in and didn't need to clean anything just yet. He realized at that particular moment he had left his squirt bottle for his demonstration at a previous apartment and hurried off.

Later, in one of those rare moments as I was sitting in the only chair we have in the living room watching television, there came another knock at the front door. My immediate thought was that here is another sales pitch. I opened the door to find a young woman with a boy in her arms who frantically asked me to call an ambulance as they did not have a telephone and her son was having a seizure. I picked up my phone and dialed 911 and told the dispatcher I needed an ambulance immediately and gave her the address. I explained that there was a young mother holding her son who needed help and that he appeared to have had a seizure. I then turned my attention back to the young woman and her son, who turned out to be my neighbor from two doors down. She told me that her four-year old son was sitting on the floor watching television and just went limp and ended up on the floor.

In minutes I heard the sirens and shortly thereafter an ambulance and fire truck arrived, and I waved them into the parking lot. Then this young woman's husband arrived home not knowing what was going on. Turns out they have a little daughter as well. Well, the paramedics got the young boy into a stretcher in the ambulance and everyone loaded up and off they went. I met my next door neighbors on either side of me, and I had the whole neighborhood outside with a bunch of folks coming up to me asking me what had happened. Everyone saw the fire truck and lights and had heard the sirens and thought that an apartment was on fire. Guess I stirred things up a bit.

Today when I came home after work there were two young boys working on a pickup truck. I went on inside the apartment when there was a knock on the door. One of the young boys asked if he could call his mom because their truck wouldn't shift into gear and they had a transmission leak. I showed him to the phone but he didn't know how to explain where he was so I talked to his mother and gave her directions. Turns out the boys were up in Indianapolis checking things out, as boys will do, when their truck's transmission quit. I worked on their truck some, and put in all of the transmission fluid that I had into their transmission. We got the truck to where it would at least go forward.

The young driver offered me all of his money which amounted to a couple of dollars for my efforts, which I declined, stating that I had a son his age and I would want someone to help him out should he ever be in a similar situation. I went back inside the apartment and got both boys a cold soda pop to drink. I told them that this was the way we helped folks out in Wyoming and I waited with them until their mother showed up.

I gave them directions on how to get back to Waverly and said goodbye. The young driver grinned and said his thanks, and off they all went. About that time, the young father of the boy with the seizure from the night before showed up and apologized for not thanking me the previous night. I shook his hand and introduced myself, as I had done with my other neighbors the previous evening. (I wrote everyone's name down so I wouldn't forget who they were.) His son is doing okay but still has a high fever.

Then I went upstairs and woke Thomas up, and off we went to Hooters for supper. The meal was good, but it was noisy. Thomas and I had plenty to eat which for me was good, considering all of the "distractions" I had to put up with there, and these last two days. I'm still trying to figure out where the "owl" part fits in—but my concentration isn't totally there.

Words

I was in the Greenwood Super Wal-Mart this morning doing my normal weekly shopping when I passed by the school supplies isle and overheard the words of one woman addressing a teenager, "Shopping for school supplies? Glad I don't have to do that no more!" (I'm happy that she doesn't either—it would have been a waste of the taxpayer's money.)

"Words" are what we live by on a daily basis and how we communicate with one another. Now, I'm usually down to earth in my speech and I try not to butcher the King's language too badly. But there seems to be more usage of "adjectives" these days in descriptive language pertaining to everyday events. I'll admit that I'm not completely in-tune with some of this descriptive language. Some of this language even leaves me mystified.

That's not to say that I can't rip off a good rendition of my own when I'm upset. I only have to listen to a few minutes of other conversations to realize what a low-life individual I can become by using the same language. I would like to keep my language more in the acceptable range than to be rude, even if it doesn't quite fit perfect form. For instance, the expression "Horse Feathers" expresses my doubts regarding something. "Yee-Ha" conveys excitement to me. To me, "When hell freezes over!" means I'm never going to see it, which for me, applies to a multitude of things. "Kiss my grits" can mean many things to many folks. Remember the one, "Up your nose with a rubber hose!". Now taken literally, the grits and the hose thing don't make a lot of sense—but the message conveyed does. Or, "I'm going to beat you like a step child". Is there a difference if you're not a step child? Because if there is a difference—I want to be one.

Then there's that feeling of helplessness conveyed in the expression, "Like pissing up a rope". I don't mean to offend anyone here—but I've felt like that on a few occasions and it does portray closely my feelings at times. The point I'm trying to make here without someone taking offense at my examples, is that "language" conveys a message, and unless you're in-tune with the latest vernacular you won't know what someone may be saying to you. You could entirely misunderstand the intended message.

Now, movies seem to be the newest form of inventiveness when it comes to language. I've learned a lot of new words watching movies. Thank goodness I was watching the movie and the events as they unfolded or taken alone, I would not have understood the meaning of the words. I find it amusing that we update our dictionaries with new words and their meanings on a regular basis. "Slang" and poor spelling have replaced most of our proper English these days. I wonder how many others have seen the lite (light)? Or am I the only one here fussing for nothing?

On the other hand, just listening to the conversations of others can be an educational experience. Makes me wonder though, if the woman who was glad that she didn't have to that "no more" was the product of our educational system or if she's just down to earth as I am.

Snipe

Many years ago when I was a young lad growing up on the farm in southern Indiana, I would often spend a night alone out in the woods beyond the back pasture underneath the stars. I would, as any boy my age, build forts, platforms in the trees and rail fences surrounding the perimeter of my camping area to keep the cattle from walking on me in the middle of the night. The woods at night without a moon are indeed dark—very dark. Even with a moon, the shadows come creeping upon one if that person is not careful.

One particular night that I remember quite well was a night in which the darkness was so intense that to walk through the woods was indeed an invitation for a collision with trees, or even worse, landing in the bottom of a ravine and remaining until morning light arrived. But the darkness was far surpassed by the night noises. I had never heard so many noises! "Things" walked the floor of the woods, twigs snapped in the dark, and other "things" scurried up trees and came to rest over my head in the branches. Owls "hooted" in the eerie quiet when all other noises ceased. Always on the ready—I never went into the woods at night without a lantern or a flashlight.

This one particular night, just as I was enjoying one of those rare uninterrupted moments of total and blissful sleep, I was awakened by a noise that I could not recognize. I clicked on my two-cell D battery flashlight and scanned the trees about me. I was sleeping on a platform built between four trees approximately five feet off the ground. I detected nothing by the light. I curled up in my blankets once more, ever watchful and sensitive towards the noise I had heard. Just as slumber reached my mind, there was the noise again, directly overhead in the branches above me.

I switched on my flashlight (we didn't have Mag lights in those days) and there above me in the branches and partly hidden in the leaves was a large creature of greenish color whose eyes shown yellow in the light. This creature had a long tail, which was wrapped around the limb it was perched upon, and I could see in the light, small claws on its feet clutching the limb, and all the while, peering intently at me with no sign of fear whatsoever. This creature then emitted the most hideous sound I had ever heard in my young life. So intense was the sound and so nerve-wracking, that I inadvertently dropped my flashlight, which fell to the ground five feet below my platform. The light stayed on, and only partially through its reflective glow could I see this creature move through the branches above me and out of my vision.

Cautiously, I climbed down my ladder to the ground below to retrieve the flashlight. Suddenly, the leaves on the ground became a flurry of motion and noise and my flashlight was knocked from where it lay, down the slight incline and to the bottom of the ravine below from where I camped. I could no longer see the light and could only estimate at what location in the ravine below that it had rolled to. Carefully in the dark I made my way back up the ladder to my sleeping platform and crawled into my blankets. I had no light and no way out until morning.

It was a very restless night, and I do not recall any additional sleep during those hours before dawn. I do remember quite well that creature's hideous sound throughout the entire night in the branches above my platform. It sounded as if this little monster was saying, "S...N...I...P...E..."

Romans

The days of the Roman Empire came to an end for various reasons. Corruption manifested itself in many governing ways while the populace became less involved in their national policy. There was a feeling of detachment, and consequently, alienation towards involvement by the people themselves. Some have even hypothesized that "lead" in plumbing may have been a cause for the illness of the wealthy class. (Only the rich could afford indoor plumbing.)

Many historians liken this nation of ours to that of the Roman Empire. But, I disagree for the most part. Realistically, I think that we as a nation are in worse shape than the Romans. We are already at that point where the populace is uninvolved with their government and has little or no say in who is elected to office. If you disagree with my analysis then ask yourself, when was the last time you knew of a poor but honest person that spoke for the people, being elected to office? In evaluating tax dollars spent, correlate the expenditure and what you paid to the actual benefits you received in return. What governmental "services" were you able to "cash in" on over the last eighteen months?

I've always theorized that taxes should never go up—but down. My reasoning is that there is more than enough money collected to fund responsible government—it's just that there isn't a responsible government. What happens to that one individual or group of individuals that takes a stand against taxation? Some experts on taxation and the law have stated that the present federal income tax system that we currently have has been unconstitutional since it was enacted.

This year many tax-paying citizens are receiving a refund check for last year's overpayment of federal income taxes. Ah, how we relish the crumbs as tokens from our governing class. People don't vote anymore—more than half of the population never casts a vote. In reality, our officials are elected by the minority of citizens. That "minority" is usually out-spoken and many of the groups that are characteristic of the "minority" have their own agenda at election time. Most people are not informed enough to make a wise decision regarding an election, nor anyone running who is wise enough to answer the call.

What we have then is a government, elected by a minority of voters whose majority doesn't care enough to vote, for politicians who can't tell the difference between a pump handle and a monkey's tail. If you don't know the difference between a pump handle and a monkey's tail, you can bet that I won't be sending you for water—or Washington D.C. Of course, the real problem of apathy in the people and in our elected officials may simply be a physical one.

Nearly everyone has indoor plumbing these days and it wasn't all that long ago that lead was used in the plumbing of our homes and other structures. Perhaps we are ahead of our time?

Where?

Asked, "Where are you from?", as I have been so many times since moving back to Indiana, causes me to pause before answering the question. It's not necessarily a mental block that I have in contemplating my answer, but rather an analysis of the question itself. My first response is to reply "Not from around here…"—which is generally correct. But what brings out my consternation is the realization that I must be from somewhere.

Most folks will respond to the question by giving the name of the town that they are presently living in—Greenwood, Martinsville, Indianapolis, Carmel, Lawrence, Gillette, and so on, if it's a "local" question. I call that an "In-State" question and response. However, if you're out and around or on vacation your response would probably be more tailored towards the state you're from or the region of that state. For me I have to sometimes go into greater depth to explain to the questioner why I can't give them a perfect answer. "Let's see—I was born in Kentucky, adopted and raised in southern Indiana, lived in Wyoming…oh yes, I have also lived in other parts of the country as well, and I have lived in Europe and Asia too. Specifically speaking, I'm not really sure where I'm from. I know where I've been though."

It's like someone asking you when you get home, "Where have you been?" Once again the answer must fit the situation. If you're a kid who is late getting home and your parent is the interrogator you have to think fast. If it's your spouse asking, you have to know three things. First, what mood is the spouse in. Secondly, were you somewhere you shouldn't have been? The third thing is, do they really want to know where you've been or is it just a conversational thing?

"Oh, out and around" is usually not a sufficient answer in either of these examples.

Then of course there is the question, "Where are you going?" This of course depends on the situation again and the questioner. Living here on the outskirts of Indianapolis, when I depart to go somewhere in this traffic my plans are not always in sync with the intended results. Of course I have clear intentions on the route I have chosen ahead of time, but with all of the road construction in this region I find that the "mine field" is moved on a daily basis.

So, let's see now…"Where are you from?", "Where have you been?", "Where are you going?"—All legitimate questions with illegitimate answers. And the amazing thing about all of those various questions is…it doesn't really matter. In the circle of life there is no beginning…and no end. Where you are from, where you have been and where you are going are all one and the same.

Plastics

Vinyl cowboys of the West and polyester businessmen of the East. Unbreakable attire…or is it? Plastics make the world go around. There's certainly some metal in both—but not as much steel. More gold and silver plated, but less iron and pewter.

There's something about texture and grain in wood. Laminated particle board lacks originality. Digital pictures are specific in subject matter. There are good photographers but few artists. I'd rather have a good canvas depicting life than I would an excellent photograph that captures the moment. "Art" today is a rare form of expressionism. Mass production with individual differences is more the norm. Take away the plastic and we're back to basics. What we previously had in our homes were products of metal, wood and glass.

Today we function with "plastic" plates, utensils, trash bags, containers, furniture, clothing, appliances, and other forms of house ware and decorative products. I like the smell and feel of leather and solid wood. I enjoy the metal "ring" of steel against steel. Canvas and pigment does more for me than enhanced photography. A book that tells a story stays with me longer than an abbreviated version of internet events. Recyclable lives are hardly worth a glance—but the "Real McCoy" stands alone.

Plastic lacks personality. Metal, wood and glass expresses individuality. There's a lot more work and effort in those individual items. A painting or simple charcoal sketch requires more effort in viewing. It makes one think. A photograph is…duh. Oh, I know that our lives are more convenient because of the advances in technology today. We expect to be comforted and pampered by industry products in our lives. A vinyl floor is easier to maintain than a hardwood floor. Polyester with a mixture of "Asian cotton" is more colorful than wool. Metal that sparkles catches the eye easier than that which is forged and hammered into shape. Interlocking tacked-back furniture mixed with modern plastics is easily produced and "designable".

I would like to sit at a table with china plates, silver utensils, glass decanters and cloth napkins. A good pot roast with vegetables from the garden, homemade bread, fresh-ground coffee and made-from-scratch pie for desert. Nothing on the table that had a food label on it previously. A table cloth covering an old wood table, and wooden chairs made by hand without a factory name. When done with my dinner and thanking my host, I could put on my wool-brimmed hat and leather coat and step out…feel the Fall in the air and go for a walk down a cobblestone path. And walk away from this synthetic life.

Importance

If asked, "What is most important in your life?" one could expect a multitude of varying answers to such a simple question. But, such a simple answer would not be sufficient in most instances. Because "life" is not simple—nor was it designed to be. Really though, try and answer the question realistically and you'll find yourself lost in the process. When I view the heavens and the earth, I am grateful for sight.

I converse with my son and daughter, and my family on this weekend visit to Elwood, Indiana and I am grateful for hearing and for speech. The weather alters and then is replaced with wind, rain and cooler temperatures as a front moves though the region and brings a multitude of new smells—for which I am also grateful. A hug or a handshake, and I realize how grateful I am for the feeling of touch. And I realize that however incomplete life seems at times, "completeness" is in the senses—and senses are the highway to the heart.

For all of my inadequacies are more than compensated by my senses. Too simple for some, but more than enough for me. A smile, a laugh, a posture or personal mannerism stays imbedded in my memory. Years from now I will always remember, as I have remembered in previous years, those particular events or situations that I have been so fortunate to have lived out. How odd, those past periods and experiences of bitterness and suffering are replaced by minutes in duration of the good and simple things in our lives. Some people continue to live out their own personal vengeance of the past, but I have accepted the past for what it has become. I no longer have the desire to become the fuel for someone's search to continue their own unhappiness. They will have to provide their own fuel and look elsewhere for sympathy, as I have too many things that I am grateful for in this life.

Material possessions are of little relevance to me but are accumulations. "Memories" are precious, and though accumulated, are never lost to age. My daughter will be visiting for only a few more days before she flies back to Colorado. My son's summer employment here in Indiana will terminate at the end of this week. He will be moving to Colorado in another week or so where he will be closer to his sister and the life he enjoys so much in the West. And their Dad...well, anyone who knows their Dad is welcomed to any multitude of guesses as to what his intentions are, and he's not saying.

"Life" is a flower, and one should nourish it from bud to blossom. I don't know how you would personally answer the question of what is most important in your life, but for me, it would be...the feeling.

Army Deaths

I sometimes wonder, in looking back on my days in the Army, whatever happened to those lives of the individual soldier or their families after death drew its veil. While in Europe, I was familiar with death on several occasions. Too many young lives lost and families forever changed. A young soldier burned beyond recognition from the overhead power lines above the railroad tracks. Another soldier just arriving in the unit who commits suicide by jumping from a smoke stack next to a power plant. An infantry soldier talking with another crew member in their personnel carrier—shot through the back by a fifty caliber round accidentally discharged by the crew behind him.

On one occasion, I accompanied the pastor as we made notification to the wife of one of our men who died coming home from field duty. I still remember the sunny day and the chopper I was flying in, that went down due to low oil pressure. A soldier is shot with a forty-five round that grazes the chin and then enters and exits through the shoulder. And I still vividly recall the bullets working their way towards me as another team mistakenly fires in my direction on a live-fire range—tracers in slow motion.

Stateside there are deaths of individual soldiers as well, in the motor pool or on field exercises. Tanks that overturn, jeeps that fall into holes in the desert, a soldier cut in half as two tanks collide. A British officer assigned to our unit whose legs are run over by a personnel carrier while he sleeps on the desert floor.

Korea held much the same in the way of deaths and injury. A young soldier with but a short time remaining overseas is working on a flat tire alongside the road when a drunken Korean runs him over. Another soldier just walking the streets is knifed to death in a Korean downtown area.

Sometimes luck prevails. On a live-fire range stateside a soldier accidentally detonates a white phosphorus grenade that showers the main gun ammo laid on the ground. I run through the dark with a fire extinguisher in my hand, as do several other team members, towards the flames hoping to extinguish them before the entire ammunition dump explode. On a dark moonless night in the middle of a live-fire exercise, my fifty caliber machine gun jams. I yell to my driver to get down—stay down! I repeat my order twice and make sure that he is out of harm's way. I release the cover on the machine gun and the bolt slams forward firing one round over the head of my driver. He is okay. Too many lives lost—too many families whose husband or father would not make it home, all because of errors. And to this day, I still think about those who are no longer here and their families whose lives were forever altered. In the Army, especially in the Combat Arms branches, there is no such feeling of complete safety—even in peacetime. That one second in time, or the moment of distraction, can bring the world to a complete halt.

A second that takes a lifetime to act itself out—and then it is all over. I thank the One above, who ensured that I did not contribute to the senseless death of another. That would be worse than death itself. And still…I will not forget.

Meadowlark

Hot and very humid here today. Of course, it was nearly always hot in the summer out West—but without the humidity. In the mountains the weather can get darn right cold in the summer. At the higher elevations it can rain and then turn to snow in August. The prairie grasses have dried up by this time of the year. What starts in May in terms of "greenery" is usually over with by July. I recall the many times where out in the Grasslands I would lounge in the shade with my dog and the only sound would be the wind in the grasses and an occasional Meadowlark song.

One of the most spectacular sights I have witnessed was up on Reno's Hill at the Custer Battlefield years ago. All of the other visitors had previously departed from the site and I was there with my family. I saw a Meadowlark land upon a large bush and begin its song. There is nothing lonelier or more uplifting than to hear the voice of that particular songbird.

This summer for the first time in so many years I never climbed a mountain nor slept out on the prairie. I never stood beside a campfire in the night nor held a hot cup of coffee in my hands as I watch the sun break the eastern sky in the morning. I was not able to play tag with my dog around the campsite in the early hours—she chasing me and then me chasing her. I did not fill my canteen from a cold mountain stream nor gaze upon the mountain meadows rich with color. I guess one could say that my life has lacked "quality" this year so far.

The traffic in this Indianapolis area is hectic and the noise is ongoing—night and day. Many times when I step outside at night I can't even see the stars or feel a breeze. I suffocate in this humid and polluted air. No sound is familiar to my ear that I might recognize as a friend to my soul. I continue to strive and adjust to this area—but I have been gone too long to assimilate into the mainstream of metropolitan life. I have taken my web site down because I have nothing of value to add to it any longer. And soon Thomas will be moving to Colorado to be back with his friends, which I think is wonderful. I would never want to prevent my children from their happiness in life. Perhaps I was mistaken in bringing him with me in our move from the West.

I want my daughter and son to live where they can see the mountains each day of their lives. I have changed my email and will no longer be using this address. Please update your email address book accordingly. I know that I will never see nor hear a Western Meadowlark here in Indiana—but the melody…is memory.

Part Three: Starting Over—Southeastern Wyoming

Back at the Cattail

Where do I begin? I am presently visiting my daughter, Amanda, here in Denver today. I talked with Thomas for a brief time on the phone this morning as well. He now lives in Fort Collins, Colorado. Thomas is about an hour and fifteen minutes away from me—Amanda is about an hour and forty-five minutes in distance.

But, back to where I begin. I moved Thomas to Fort Collins back in August where he is now sharing an apartment with his high school buddy. He is enjoying every minute there. Myself—I am living the life of a cowboy once more on the ranch where I worked thirty-three years ago. I went there for a visit and I was hired on immediately as the previous hand was thrown from a horse and broke his arm. That man has not returned since, and I was asked to take his place.

I now have the same horse but "Foxy" has only given me problems a few times thus far. I have read all of your email and I keep in contact with Amanda by cell phone. She is my secretary for my email. As for my computer—I no longer have access to it as I gave the entire system to Thomas. Today was the first time I've been able to personally read my email here in Denver. My heart has been touched by the email I have received from those who have written and I apologize for not have the capability to respond. My life these last several weeks has consisted of cattle, horses and hard work.

So, I only have a few hours here before I drive back to the ranch north of Cheyenne and I will therefore simply send word to all at the same time and hope that I do not offend anyone in doing so. My work day begins before dawn and ends when dark—six days a week, at least. This morning after chores were done I left for Denver and I will return to the ranch again tonight. The last couple of weeks I have spent in the saddle moving cattle from one range to another. I don't have a personal phone other than my cell phone which I only have on when I make a call. But I do have an address for anyone who wishes to write.

Living in Indiana was very tough for me. I missed the wide open spaces. I was very fortunate to have been able to visit my family and I do miss everyone in the Indiana and Kentucky areas—more than you will ever know. I want to thank each of you for all that you did for me and my son Thomas while we were there. I only wish that I had the time to personally write everyone. With Thomas moving to Colorado and Amanda already there I could not live so far apart from my children. I can't live their lives for them, but I don't want to live a life without them either.

So now my days are once more filled with the wind in the sage, the snow-capped mountains in the distance, the creak of saddle leather and the sky as my ceiling. The stars at night are my canopy and the coyotes my music. And if I don't get busted-up on this crazy horse, I just might be able to get myself "broke" back in after six to eight hours a day riding.

But always, I remember those that I love, wherever you may live, and know that my thoughts are with you all. Special thanks to Donna and Larry, Mother, Cheri and Darrell, Sandy, Bernie and Geniva, Don and Jewel, Jim and Terry, Deborah, and Dennis. You were there when I need you the most.

Orphans

A typical day? I'm usually up by 5:20 in the morning and out the bunkhouse door by six o'clock. It's dark and cold now at that time of the day. I walk over to one of the buildings and climb aboard the ATV, start it up and across country I go in search of the cow, four calves and two steers to bring back to the corrals. The cow, "Alphie", I milk by hand. I feed cake to the four calves and two steers. Three of the calves I give milk to from the milk bucket.

"Clown", the one calf, gets no milk bucket. He was born in late spring and his mother was found dead out on the prairie. Clown is an orphan. We call him Clown because he is part Hereford and part Angus, and has a black ring around one of his eyes. He doesn't seek attention and is a loner. But he is doing well and growing along with the other three calves. There are well over three-hundred and fifty other calves that live out on the prairie and that have their mothers with them.

Around the 14th of October we'll have to round up all of the other calves and their mothers so that we can give the calves their second vaccinations. It's an all day affair moving over seven hundred calves and heifers to another part of the range for the vaccinations. Fence boundaries are at least a mile apart in distance here and there's lots of miles to cover. Riding all day on horseback and cutting cattle can wear one out. This coming week we will be hauling more cake for the winter feeding of the cattle. We load three trucks at a time with around seven tons per truck consisting of fifty pound bags. All total, we'll load and haul around one-hundred tons of cake to the two ranches for starters. Then we unload the cake again.

Yesterday I was out working on the barbed wire fence that encloses the meadow where we will put the calves this winter. Out by myself along the fence line, stretching wire and digging holes for fence posts—repairing as I went along. Two days ago I was again out by myself taking care of the numerous windmills, scratchers, mineral and salt for the cattle in five different ranges.

I enjoy the wind and the open sky overhead. There are no human noises or any other habitation nearby out there, just the cattle in particular locations. Way off to the west I can see the Laramie Mountains. Out to the southwest I can make out the outline of the Rockies. I know that my son and daughter are out that way somewhere.

Late afternoon I seek out the cow, four calves and the two steers once more. By six-thirty it's time for supper. Night comes and as the sun turns the horizon to red and pink, the coyotes begin their calling. They stir up the two ranch dogs, who bark in response to the coyote howling. The wind picks up as the sun drops below the western hills and the stars turn up their intensity. Tomorrow the process and hard work begins all over again, but this time of the day is indeed a blessing. And I'll see Clown once more in the morning light and make sure he made it safely through another night.

Orphans touch my heart. P.S. Visiting my daughter in Denver today and leaving for the ranch this evening. Sundays are the only days I have to rest after chores are done in the morning.

Fall at the Ranch

The Cottonwood trees have released their golden leaves and the cattails have turned into yellow stalks. The wind is gently cooler and the nights are cold. I am reminded of the world of reality when I visit my daughter in Denver, as I am doing today.

These last several weeks have found me de-horning cattle—and I am blood splattered. We have branded cattle and a few bulls and the smell of burnt hair and hide fill my nostrils. Cattle have been moved to their winter ranges—closer to the ranch. The one ranch hand that broke his ribs when thrown from his horse is now gone, replaced by another man. Yesterday while moving bulls to another range, one young lady who was assisting us was thrown from her horse. I found her standing on a hill, her horse far away. When I rode up to her she didn't know where she was, what she was doing there, or how she had gotten there. Amnesia had taken its toll when her head had bounced off the ground when she was thrown. She rode with me for about an hour until her memory came back, and her horse was recovered for her.

"Reality" is something taken for granted. Today, I tried several times to utilize my Yahoo email but to no avail. So, I had to switch to Hotmail instead. My everyday reality is with the land and the climate, not computers. Folks live in this concrete world and call it reality. My daughter and my son, who is visiting from Ft. Collins today, have all the interests of what mankind has invented in this glittering city. Their highway is their path to reality, while my path is my reality.

Turning off the various windmills and cleaning out the water tanks, moving the steers in to feed each morning, milking the cow morning and evening, repairing vehicles, being careful not to let a horse get the best of me as we ride down a steep and rocky hill side, watching my back as I move cattle into one corral and into the chutes so I won't be slammed into the rails—little bits of reality as reminders of how fragile the body and mind are. The only time I have to check my email is when I visit Denver, and there may not be another visit for some time.

The snow will be coming to stay soon and with it the cold. The holidays, for some, will be here shortly as well…yet each day at the ranch is a constant reality check for me. I know now that what exists in our society can no more hold my attention than the latest news event. My world is without the hype and glitter. My "gold" is that of Nature's colors that surrounds me on a daily basis. It's a "reality" I can live with.

Part Four: Searching for Home—Back to the Midwest

Trip to Indiana

Life moves me down paths that I have often walked before, and yet the landscape is different with each journey. I see things that have been there forever but are viewed from a different perspective each time I stumble the same route. Perhaps it is the light, or that the shadows cast a different image that never remains the same.

Wyoming has been cold and gusting with the winter cold. I think of where "home" is for me at two o'clock in the afternoon and my thoughts drift back to Indiana—childhood dreams that remain to this day. I see the frigid scenery of Omaha, Nebraska roll by my windows at midnight and I wonder if this old pickup truck could possibly take me further east. Still dark and so cold—Iowa surrounds me as I drive further east in search of both the known and unknown.

By six o'clock in the morning I am still driving in the cold, as I reach the Mississippi River and dawn's overcast arrival depicts the expansive water course below me. By mid-morning I am clinching the steering wheel and trying to maintain a straight course through the snow and ice in Peoria, Illinois—mindful of the semi tractor-trailer rigs that are jack-knifed and cars that are off the road around me. I am very tired now—I've been driving alone since two o'clock Tuesday afternoon.

I wish for company—someone to talk with and to share thoughts with. Conversation to keep me from falling asleep at the wheel. Each stop along the way consists of refueling, oil, cleaning the windshield, checking the antifreeze and checking the transmission and tires. I grab another Honey Bun roll and a hot cup of coffee at the gas station and climb back into this beater of a truck, praying that the starter will turn over the engine so I can get warm again. Down to the on ramp and I'm done with another pit stop for another 300 miles or three or more hours of steady driving.

I humor myself when I begin to tire at the wheel by singing aloud out the open window. After a few short verses of a cowboy song or two I have awakened myself and the entire population of whatever town I am driving through to the extent where I hear only the howling of dogs in the background as I depart.

I reach the Indiana state line by eleven o'clock Wednesday morning and finally arrive "home" on then farm by one o'clock in the afternoon (Mountain Time); twenty-three hours driving time—one thousand one hundred and eight miles as I pull into the driveway. I'm tired but not beat yet. I stop and try and remember my address now. Sounds familiar—and so have many of the previous paths taken before.

My ranching and cowboy days are over, for now, and I set my mind towards rest for the present and possible new encounters for the future. I am more comfortable on the road I think than I am staying too long in one place. "Perspective" is enriched when the scenery changes often. Look at something too long it will become a blur. Look away and then look at it again and it becomes a different picture.

I wonder how the boys are doing back there on the ranch in Wyoming. Right now, the only thing I know for sure is that I am not there with them.

Old Home

This morning I moved down to the main house here on the farm and I am staying with Mother. I am utilizing my sister Cheri's computer for my email messages. Her home is located on the other side of the town of Martinsville. I get over this direction once in awhile to check my email and to visit with her as well. It's a pretty day here in southern Indiana today—though a wee bit chilly. I'm not use to the higher humidity—yet.

I do miss life at the ranch and all of the wonderful folks there. (Seems as if I have spent the last year or so, on the road to somewhere, never knowing for sure whose doorstep I will visit next.) I am looking for employment in this region close to "home" but I am enjoying life as well in the meantime. I am grateful to all who have taken their time to make me feel at home—without regard to their own situation. The saying goes that a rolling stone gathers no moss in this neck of the woods. I've checked—and I have found no "green" anywhere on this body of mine. That could be good, or bad, depending on one's definition of "green".

I don't know that the term "Considerations" is always appropriate when I send out my emails—but I will stick with that term. I've been writing my "Considerations" for well over a year now to many folks and the inquiry has been

"When are going to write a book about your experiences?" Well, I'm still collecting and saving those that I have written and I will eventually place them in a book for the general public to read. In the meanwhile, this small audience gets first pick and editorial rights. Chop, chop! How do I incorporate the mesas and the mountains with cropland and housing developments?

It's not the destination, but the road traveled, that determines who we are and what we become. The exciting thing is that the roads I have traveled have passed through so many wonderful people lives, like you. When I view the passing scenery through the windshield throughout this great land of ours, I always do a "reality check". In other words, I look out the nearest window at the highway passing underneath my vehicle—watching the pavement zip by at incredible speed and then I look upwards once more at the stationary landscape. I am reminded that as life tends to "zip" by—the destination always remains the same for me.

Rat

Dusk. The last rays of light dwindle to the darkness of the stalks in the corn field. Three dark smudges up by the hill. I wait—and the shadows move ever so slightly in the center of the field. I walk silently forward and stop. The smudges are joined by other shadows and my eyes adjust to the gathering dark. And then recognition—Odocoileus virginianus. I retreat to inside the farm house, gather up my binoculars, and return to my spot at field's edge as quickly as possible. Now I see them moving not more than fifty yards away and I count eleven in front of me. I recount again…eleven, Whitetail Deer. This includes the three fawns staying close to their mothers. All are browsing the corn field stumps as they move slowly westward through the dark.

In the daylight I check the rat trap I've place by the outside window to the cellar. For several nights I've heard the loud scratching noise of the animal in the wall above my head. The trap is gone. I search the yard outside—nothing. I dread the journey to the dark and musky underground beneath the house. Flashlight in hand, down the steps I go in search of the creature. I step carefully through the mud and rock outcrops but see and hear nothing. I return outside again to where I had set the trap and discover the blood marks. Again I return to the cellar, and find two small blood spots on a small rock in the mud. I'm on the trail…when I notice the light's reflection on the edge of the trap underneath the water heater. I can't see the business end of the trap—so I poke it with a yardstick.

The trap leaps outward and comes to life. Black eyes stare in anger at me as the rat thrashes around carrying the trap. I leave and return quickly with a shovel.

One hard smack sends the rat into total rage. I gather him and the trap into the shovel and race up the cellar steps. He takes the trap and jumps off the shovel at the top of the stairs and lands on the carpet. Enough! I reach down and with shovel and gloved-hand carry the two outside. Two sharp blows with the shovel and the rat has met his match. I throw him into the grass.

The wind goes where it wishes. The black and gray clouds roll in from the southwest bringing the rain and thunder before them. Turbulence overhead as the lower clouds are pushed in various angles. I hear the honking, and look upward. The two "V's" are destroyed—the geese calling out to one another as they struggle to maintain a semblance of beauty...to no avail. The gusts turn them...and so they resign themselves to the direction of Nature. Better to survive first, and worry about the beauty of the dance later. The rain finally drives me inside the old farm house.

I swat at a spider...then a fly. I begin to read and the little lady-bug-type beetles begin to dive-bomb my pages. I flick them away with my fingers, like a sling shot. They have successfully broken my concentration. Little reminders of who we are and where we fit into the nature of things. All these...great and small. I was never invited. As a gracious guest I have accepted most of their conditions.

Politics

Mother and I rarely completely agree on any topic. She's a "radical conservative" and I'm a "liberal radical". At times we watch the television news together or "discuss" political opinions. Some instances she even asks me what I think regarding a certain topic. (Of course, to think I would have full liberty to expound completely to a question she asks is wishful thinking.) I am branded by her as belonging to this "generation" of dismay and decay. (Silently, of course, I reflect upon some of her generation's teachers in my life.) We do have spirited conversations though.

I have resigned myself to the fact that no matter my position on any topic, my thoughts are a doomed process. She asks me, "What's wrong with drilling for oil and laying pipeline up there in Alaska? It's wilderness that nobody sees anyway. Besides, we need the oil!" Ah yes—here we go...fire in the hole! I explain that we could be environmentally safe in the production and transportation of most of the oil there—but that's not the point. "Well! What's the point!" she asks. I explain that the problem is not the oil—but our use. "Well—you tell me what all of those oil tankers from Japan are doing up there! I saw them when I visited there!" she replies. I explain that those tankers are taking our oil to Japan where they fuel their industry to produce the goods that we buy here in America.

She raises her voice to a new level and exclaims, "And that's why there are fewer jobs here at home!" Exactly…Mother. Fair Trade Act, etc. etc. I explain that it's not about "jobs"—it's about "money". That's why it's financially better for auto companies to sell you a big truck, SUV or a car with a big engine. The companies make more money per unit at the higher sale. They don't care what the price of gas is…or how much oil is left. They don't care where the vehicle is produced either. The bottom line is a bigger return—and their responsibility to the stock owned by shareholders. I explained that the oil in Alaska isn't the point—it's the digression. "We'll just use that oil up and then have to drill somewhere else again. In the meanwhile, that Alaskan wilderness is gone forever." Enron is just the tip of corporate America's problems. Just because other companies have better accounting practices and are more "accountable" doesn't mean they're any more honest. Just means they haven't been caught. And who does Congress and the Supreme Court think they are? "Representatives" of the people investigating anything and everything to cover up their own private world. (When was the last time that "We the People" voted Congress a pay raise?) The President is a one-man show and a token of the Republic. He can't accomplish anymore that the other parts of government, but we expect him to anyway…

Ah—now I have a Mother-induced headache, I'm mad at myself and the world in general because I can't place the blame on anyone, and I'm still a member of that "give me" generation. I haven't solved a damn thing and I have agreed upon even less. I go back to my reading and contemplate that perhaps watching cartoons on the boob tube rather than news, is better for one's health.

Big Brother

Will Rogers is quoted to have said that he "never met a man he didn't like…" Bill Clinton, on the other hand, is rumored to have mentioned that he "never met a woman that he didn't like…" If I had my choice as to who was actually telling the truth I guess it would be with Clinton, even if Will Rogers was, without a doubt, the more honorable of the two.

Looking back in time, there have been many examples in recorded histories that are not truthful explanations of what really took place. Having lived a portion of that era that is now being taught to today's youth, I can testify to the inaccuracy of recorded history, as could my previous generation, and the generations before them. "History" is what writer wishes the reader to believe. And while I am tremendously interested in various aspects of history, I can find fault with what has been written for today's reader. A number of events that have been recorded for all times still do not ring true. For example, John F. Kennedy was not a great president, but just got lucky in world events that could have otherwise been a global disaster. Oswald did not act alone in JFK's death but instead received direction and support to accomplish the overall mission. One can't question a dead man, can we Mr. Ruby?

UFO's do exist and they're not really Unidentified Flying Objects, as we label them. (I know who they really are, but I'm not telling.) Our government knows what is really going on even if their public announcements indicate otherwise.

Really though, our government knows more about you than you realize. Every time one of your credit cards is scanned for a purchase that magnetic strip on the back is providing information to the card company, the federal government, and...I won't mention who the third party is on the receiving end. It's not just one magnetic strip, folks. ANYTHING you do on the internet today can be tracked, as well as your phone calls (including cell phone), grocery cards (i.e. Marsh, Kroger, CVS, etc.), and the programs you watch on cable or dish, or the OnStar option in your new vehicle that pinpoints your exact location every time you drive somewhere.

Now, with all of this available "Big-Brother-is-watching" technology one would think that we could at least get History right. Wrong. "News" is influenced and even written and directed by Big Brother. Not exactly state-owned, but not independent either. The "masses" are led in the direction their government wants them to go. We are really no different than our Arab brothers and sisters whose governments accomplish the same thing in their own countries. What I'm saying is that real History is more of a belief than it is a reality. The things that we know to be true deep within, however unproven or expounded upon by History are really more accurate. This will be my last "Considerations" for the immediate future, as I no longer have access to a workable computer.

Peanut Butter

Peanut butter and jelly. They go together—like death and taxes. Yesterday I took wings and toured the immediate surrounding area. I visited Nashville, Indiana (over in Brown County) and walked into a variety of quaint shops along the streets of this small town. I enjoyed seeing the artist's work exhibited in paintings, glass, and metal—and, visiting the town folks as well. Original.

When I departed I headed down State Road 46 to Bloomington, intent on driving through the campus of Indiana University. I arrived just as the university students were leaving their classes for the lunch hour. People were everywhere! Some students were sitting upon the short walls—reading. Some were walking with their backpacks to their next class, or to lunch. Others were jogging in shorts and T-shirts, staying in shape. And there I was, cruising along in the old ranch truck, trying to keep from rubber-necking myself to death looking at all the pretty young ladies.

I had half a thought of doing some research on the differences in GPA's (grade point average) between the male and female student populations there at the university. (My theory was that the females' GPA would be much higher than the males, simply because the male population would be unable to concentrate in this type of environment.) Anyway, there I am, cruising among the BMWs and Mercedes with the student population.

None of the students paid any attention to these classic vehicles, but I got all kinds of looks. I think it had something to do with that GMC ranch-type beater truck design and me cruising with my windows down and Garth Brooks belching his latest hit out the truck windows. (I've installed a CD/radio player in the beast.) Or, it could just be my appearance—blue jeans, cow-kickin' boots and a baseball cap that said "Justin Boots…American Made Boots" on the front. Obviously, I didn't fit in with the college scene.

As I passed through the academic crowds I could hear in the background words to the effect, "Holy Moly…what the hell was that…?" Well, I'm an original. Unlike the BMWs and the Mercedes I'm not imported—no sir! I'm American made! The genuine article, one-of-a-kind, handcrafted, the "Real Thing", Made in America!

Anyway, a couple of days ago I decided to visit one of the local video stores here in Martinsville so that I could rent some movies for my Mother. I had to become a member first, and I had to fill out their application before I could rent their movies. So I filled out their application. Typical stuff—name, address, phone number etc. Then they wanted to who my employer was; phone number, social security number and so on. Well, I didn't provide a social security number and as for employment I just wrote "Retired". With my personal appearance and the questions answered correctly I received complete understanding, and I was now a member. I took my movies and left.

When one puts the word "Retired" down, that places you in a different category (actually, I'm not retired, maybe moth-balled). But when I state "Retired", that means I work when I want to work. Kind of like Union Labor. The way I figure it, I can't avoid death or taxes. I can, however, avoid work. I might as well enjoy life in the meantime. Like peanut butter and jelly.

Library

As I sit here in the Morgan County Library this beautiful and sunny morning, going over my email and making notes to myself, I pause to reflect on particular items here in Indiana that have captured my attention recently. (At my age, anything that captures my attention is relevant!) For example, I can't recall the last time when this country did the old time—change and "sprung forward" that I didn't comply. Here in this part of Indiana we don't touch our clocks either in the fall or spring. So, I didn't have to adjust anything—not even my body. Scary! Now the fact that this part of the country doesn't adjust to the new time change either makes this part of Hoosier Land the most backward in terms of "progress" or the most "forward" in terms of relativity. What it means to me personally is that now there is only a one hour difference between here and the West.

Now, I don't want to sound too technical but for all of the time geeks out there I've got news for you. Changing the clocks didn't alter sunrise and sunset times. As a matter of fact, the earth is still spinning at the same speed as before and the fact that we still see the sun in the morning and the stars at night causes me to breathe a sigh of relief, no matter what time it is.

Indiana drivers like to personalize the license plates here. For an extra twenty-five dollars, which goes to a special fund, you can get a license plate for schools, the environment, universities etc. There are all kinds of personal license plates as well—most of which are in some personal code that means nothing to anyone else except the owner of the vehicle. Duh! Anyway, there's only one personalized plate that grabs my goat whenever I see one. It's the environmental plate. I mean come on—for an extra twenty-five bucks does that person feel that they are more entitled to pollute the environment than someone else? (I haven't seen any of these environmental plates on an old beater, by the way.) Figure up what it cost to manufacture the vehicle, the pollution it spews out, and the self-centered character of the vehicle owner of being better than us brought-up-from-poverty-to-dirt-folks, and one has to wonder. I know their heart is in the right place, but their mind is where one needs a flashlight to see up there.

One last "dig" regarding another observation. Taxes. This is a state of taxes—unless you're rich. I pay federal tax, state tax, county tax and other sales taxes. If I figured all the taxes I pay and the more "bang for buck" it should bring I would have exploded a long time ago. In reality, this state's taxation and expenditure system is beyond my realm of understanding. The only thing that I do understand is that the state government, like the federal government, is not held accountable for its expenditures. (I'd like to have one of their line-of-credits!) I'm working my way towards a higher form of frustration level. I think I'll go home now and take a "Chill Pill" and drink some coffee…from Columbia.

Terror Times

I have this lousy feeling. At times I am sick of the "news", if one can really call it that. "Re-hashing" and personal agendas are more descriptive. I'm sick of politics too. I'm neither a Republican nor a Democrat—but an Independent. (So much for anyone I vote for getting into office.) In 1965 our Special Forces were in Viet Nam as advisors helping to keep Charlie in place. We had a chance then but…we blew it for the next ten years. We lost, just like we did in Korea. Now we label our conventional ground troops in Afghanistan as "Special Forces"—and we will lose again.

We called the Taliban and the al-Qaida the "Freedom Fighters" twenty years ago, when they were fighting the Soviets. Now they are our enemy because of 9-11 and the Twin Towers. We are fat, dumb and happy Americans and still cannot comprehend that we will never win using conventional forces in an unconventional war. We will, however, win every battle only to lose that war. And in doing so we will stir up every bordering nation with our threatening antics towards the use of our nuclear weapons. Great!

I hope that by now I have offended some folks. Let's look at some specifics. Back when the Army was changing its head gear to the black beret I felt that it was wrong to take the Ranger's color and adapt it to the whole army. My opinion didn't matter though. And to believe that all the ground forces in Afghanistan are "Special Forces" is a lie. (Again, my opinion doesn't matter.) To think, for example, that the 10th Mountain Division from "sea-level" New York State is a "mountain" division gets me laughing (but folks believe that too). Our high-tech military looks like a bunch of pack mules with their huge ruck sacks on their backs. You may ask, "How does today's soldier fight effectively going into battle with the kitchen sink attached to his back?" The answer is obvious—he doesn't.

I'm not critical of the real grunts, but I detest the politicians and high brass types that turn our fighting forces into jackasses. To this day Americans still do not understand guerilla warfare. To fight guerillas you must become one—thus, Special Forces. A conventional army can never defeat a guerilla force anymore than we can defeat a terrorist attack. (I feel sorry for those who lost loved ones during 9-11 but feel even worse for those who believed in their own govern-ment.) We talk the talk but never seem to walk the walk.

Killing guerillas or terrorists is a personal thing. If one cannot stand to be splattered with gore, to become a stinking and filthy animal that thinks only in terms of bathing in blood, and to scream with delightful frenzy of killing his opponent…then he or she probably doesn't have what it takes to win. I don't have a computer and I discontinued my cell phone service. I don't really need either one.

"Life" is the flesh and blood, the pulse of the heart, the flicker of the eyes, the emotions following the trail of the soul. A conversation, a gentle touch, to seek the depths of another person's vision…are more important to me than email. The term, "United States" I have found to be an oxymoron. We are no more united than we are the same. We either value ourselves for whom we are, or suffer for what we will become. If we don't have the heart to fight for life, then we must accept our own destiny.

Jobs

Having left the hotel business for a week now, I am presently working for PMI (Personnel Management, Inc.) wherever they send me—which currently is the Schulte Corporation where we make shelving and racks for contractors. I work in a noisy, very hot (over 100 degrees) and dirty plant each evening, and finally make it back to the farm by a quarter-till-one in the morning. By then I have consumed gallons of water and several Mountain Dews in the process of sweating myself to death. The only thing I want at one o'clock in the morning is a cold beer and sleep.

So this morning after I had awakened and my Mother had asked how the night had gone—I told her. She asked me, "Do you think you'll ever find a job you like?" (I told her I didn't want to start an argument right after getting up in the morning.) Anyway, that got the gears grinding away. But truthfully, I'll never find a "job" that I'll like. I don't mind working—but I detest "jobs". I've had a lot of jobs in my lifetime as I'm sure many others have. But only a few occupa-tions that have been what I call "work" where I found what I was doing actually resulted in a sense of accomplishment. One was when I was working as a service technician for Western Water, Inc., and the other was working as a ranch hand. All the other occupations were "jobs". No matter what the pay—if it was a job it sucked. If it was work, it was rewarding (but not necessarily always fun).

I've found out that money helps, but doesn't make a damn bit of difference if it comes from a job. The other important ingredient in work is whom you're working for. If you like the folks you work with and for, that can greatly determine if you're doing a job, or working. (I've worked for some folks who were great but unfortunately it was a "job".) I look back at these last couple of years in my life and what I've been doing. It certainly wasn't making any money. Last year around this time I had lost my house, my wife, and my dog. (I miss my dog.) Except for the brief vacations I had working at Western Water, Inc. and at the Cattail Ranch; life has evolved around jobs back here in the Indiana Sweat Shops. I call them "Sweat Shops" because they treat you like an idiot, pay you next to nothing, and require you to do everything that they won't do themselves.

I always enjoy hearing someone's opinion about what it's like to work here in Indiana. Especially when that person has not worked a job in say, the last twenty years or more. Not only are they are not knowledgeable about jobs, they aren't even marketable for a job themselves. (They can still expound proficiently regarding jobs though.) Here in southern Indiana most honest folks work at below the poverty level (*Indianapolis Star*—May 15, 2002)—unlike those in the greater Indianapolis areas. Those folks who want a better paying job have to commute to Indianapolis each day and then turn around a drive back home. It's bad enough driving forty or more miles to Indianapolis each day—but to a job! I figure if I have to work in a Sweat Shop and live in the poverty area of the state, I might as well drive to Bloomington and back instead. (At least it's better scenery.)

No, jobs just suck. "Work" may not be a bundle of fun, but it's much better than a job! The last most important criteria in work, besides whom you're working for, and sense of accomplishment, is if you can speak in a positive manner about what it is you have been doing. If it's a "job", then there's nothing positive to talk about. But I at least know this much. If I have been doing a "job"—I am positively going to talk about it!

Part Five: A Cowboy's Heart—Home in Wyoming

Drought

Drought. It's a harsh term that turns the land barren. Here in this portion of Wyoming it's probably the worst in a hundred years. What little grass remains is dry and brittle. Scattered thunderstorms without moisture, and parched wind. Survival is essential.

This is haying time here at the ranch. It's the time of the year when one takes inventory of food for the livestock for the winter months—and unless the rains come soon there will be no turning around. Beef prices continue to decline as more cattle head to the markets. The other day I observed two mule deer and four wild turkeys while traveling through the eastern portion of the irrigated meadow area. Wildlife close to a still-available water source.

When the first pioneers traveled the trails westward to California and Oregon territories, this area of the country was given but little thought for a home. Regions of present Wyoming were considered desert—something to overcome in passing on their way. No person in their right mind would consider settling down here in this barren, unforgiving country...especially when word of the lush country awaited them over the mountains. Hurry—push hard...overcome the mountains before the first snows. But first, get through this area of Wyoming by any route—the Mormon Trail, the Oregon Trail, the Overland Trail...and keep going.

Those pioneers that eventually made this area their home were a hardy breed. Times were never especially easy, and were usually tough on everyone. It took a special quality of individual to understand this land and to see through tough times. Descendents of those early pioneers are still here, with the same character-istics of tenacity and fortitude.

"The Cowboy State" still lives up to its name here in Wyoming. It's not just an area, than it is a "state" of mind. What runs deep here is that no matter the weather or the conditions, one still lives with the land. And if present times are severe, you adapt to the severity until the better times return…and they always do. Because if there were no "better times" there would have been no pioneers. Those that quickly continued their journey westward through this "desert" country in search of their paradise left behind a land that others more fortunate than they, were to appreciate for generations to come.

In the thirty-four years between my first visit to this high plains region and the present, I have been broken and busted-up a few times, but the body has always healed itself. That's the beauty of youth. Like this land, I've always recovered. Like this region's spirit, the music of optimism still flows within me. Humor is an antidote for the heart, and the heart is big medicine for the body. But the soul is what keeps things in harmony.

Riding for the Brand

Horse, saddle, rider. The Cavalry method of ingraining in the young trooper the sequence of care. The horse was the primary means of transportation and the first to be cared for. Anyone who has walked great distances knows the value of hoof power. Second in priority was the saddle (and equipment) necessary for insuring that the horse and rider could go the distance at moment's notice. And last was the rider (and the brains of this outfit). If he was a good trooper he had the intellect to realize the importance of priority.

Too many "managers" in today's world lack the intelligence to be leaders. They neither care for the horse or its saddle, and those in upper management have no regard for their riders. When I was in the Cavalry I detested the term "manager". Anyone can become a manager, but few are leaders. What distinguishes the manager from a leader is example. Few managers lead by example–but all leaders are at the front, or in harm's way. All leaders take responsibility for their actions and the welfare of the horse, the saddle and their riders. Managers delegate from authority. Leaders get their hands dirty and share the work load of their subordinates while maintaining their vision of the mission at hand. The leader will not ask what he cannot or will not do himself. Managers don't care about individual pride or other comrades in the unit. (That's what they were "taught".) Managers don't care about team spirit but are intent on keeping everyone in their place.

However, the most significant difference between a manager and a true leader is bull shit. That's right—I said bull shit. See, managers are full of it, and true leaders just won't put up with any of it. There's really no difference between the military and civilian side of doing a mission or one's job. Anyone whose been to more than one round-up knows that managers don't lead by example, delegate responsibility in case something goes wrong, never get their hands dirty nor share an equal work load (or danger), or could care less about the spirit of the individual. Managers care only about their job. Leaders care about the mission—and everything that makes the mission possible. Horse, saddle, rider.

Lastly and most importantly is pride. A true leader takes pride in his work—and makes it the best, based upon available resources and time allowed. Out West, pride took form in "riding for the brand". That meant the cowboy was proud of who he was and what he did for a living. He was proud of the outfit he rode for, was compassionate towards fellow cowhands, shared in all tasks of the work at hand—rode hard…and played hard. And if the cowboy didn't have pride it was only because he felt he had not done enough towards achieving the task at hand and had let others down in the process. He was a leader, even when working for others. What managers will never understand is that in trying to maintain an upper hand they can never remove pride from an individual unless that particular individual lets them. No one can take another's pride unless they surrender it.

So, whether you're a desk jockey or a laborer, a doctor or a teacher, or just a plain cowpoke—take pride in what you do…and "ride for the brand". I'll guarantee you that the last "round-up" will sort the managers from the leaders. See you there, partner.

The Beast

Dust clouds on the far horizon tell of a coming storm as the clouds change from slate to black, and the white wisps streak beneath, painting strands that intertwine the landscape with the sky. The cold shutters forth in gusts that rip the air and finds openings in the clothing of the bundled figure as the horse heads towards the nearest butte and away from the wind. Snow spits in hard pebbles, rattling off the saddle and begins to coat the horse's mane.

The ride has been hard—over two hundred miles across this high open plains country. Days and nights mixed as if one, and always the landscape rolling slowly beneath, but never the same. Nothing has been quite like it was before this journey. Only weeks ago found this same individual struggling to live after the encounter in the mountains with the "Being". That's what the local tribe's legend had named the beast of those mountains. Intrigued, this man had sought out the truth of this local lore—fact or fiction, he would find out himself the truth to these stories that the elders spoke around the fires at night.

And so he had gone to the region in the mountains that was home to these tales. The first night as he lay upon the ground by the fire he had heard a roar that echoed throughout the valley, then died in the whispering of the Ponderosa needles on the wind overhead. Morning broke cold and misty and the ground damp. Drinking his coffee beside the fire he was conscious that something was watching him. Deep within the dark shadows of the surrounding hills branches broke and the eagles screamed their warning of impending doom, yet the man would not leave.

Three more days he traveled on horseback into the gloom and further into the mountain valley and still there was nothing tangible—only that same feeling and uneasiness. But something was there. Something was watching his progress and came closer to his fire each evening.

On the fourth night while sitting by his makeshift fire a dark shadow loomed just outside the glow of the burning logs. Not a sound it made, but it presented itself as it rose from the ground and stood upon its hind legs, fur-covered and with large antlers, gleaming eyes and twitching nose. And the roar that followed surpassed anything the man had ever heard. A bone-chilling sound that began as a roar and ended as a high-pitched screech, echoing throughout the darkened valley. Mammoth—towering ten feet, its head and antlers reaching up into the lower branches of the pines. Thump...thump...thump–it moved from the shadows into the glowing light, and presented its form for what it truly was, the "Being".

The man reached for his rifle, but too late, as this creature quickly snatched the weapon and tossed it into the darkness. And then, without premonition the creature appeared to smile in its most animalistic manner, turned and thumped away into the darkness.

And now weeks later, as horse and human dredged their way across these open plains in the snow and cold...away from those very mountains of the encounter, the man pondered how his tribal brothers would receive his tale. This creature of prehistoric proportions still living in present-day Wyoming.

The man knew that his stature would remain with this tribe, what with his concurrence of their legendary tale of this beast in the mountains, and many more stories would ensue from his own sighting of this creature. But...how should he explain the beast's smile? Would others doubt this part of his story? Few individuals have had the opportunity to view what he had seen that night. So large and powerful, but with a sense of humor at the innocence of mankind. Who would believe—a smiling...Jackalope!

The Wind

The wind is my companion wherever I go. Like all close companions it can be bothersome at times. Concentration is broken when it won't cease and one is trying to fix mind with the matter at hand–like a mate that won't shut-up. Other times it is a blessing that brings new breath to a stale situation, and life changes accordingly to the new weather fronts that it brings forth.

It cares little for sound that it disperses to the four corners of the earth. It can be music, or a roar, depending upon its mood. Sometimes it is a breeze that caresses, and sometimes ceaseless slapping that chaps the exterior. On a summer day it can feel hot and dry. Winter nights it will cut deep and find one's weakness in nature.

Wyoming wind is a special kind of wind. Most of the time it finds its way over the mountains, down through the passes and across the meadows, over the foot hills skirting the pines, whisking across the prairie grasses and rocky outcrops, singing between the barbed wire and river bottoms—to a place we call home. But the wind has no home. Always traveling from and to distant places it is not interested in staying. Like a visitor, it brings forth new tidings as it passes through—spinning new yarns about where it has been and its plans for the future, pausing just long enough to let you know of its arrival, then departure, as it deposits portions of accumulations it has gathered along the way. Wind seeks resistance. It tosses itself against obstacles that it may not overcome initially. But it has endurance. The same wind that fills one's sails on the river of life can flatten mountains over time.

It brings life—from seeds to rain and snow. Sometimes it can be twisted to an extreme that brings destruction. One cannot "hear" the wind–only the resistance can be heard. This conductor of the symphony can fill my ears with melody or my eyes with grit. The sweetness of the sage in the springtime here differs from the pungent odor of industrial smoke in the metropolitan areas–all carried by the same traveler.

As a resource, the wind is beneficial in generating energy for mankind without depletion of the earth's materials. Working smarter and not harder should be a goal for humanity. Stewardship of the land requires responsibility in decisions regarding usage. It also involves deviation from the norm. Oil, coal and gas industries here in Wyoming are big business for those involved in the extraction and deportation of these resources. Riding roughshod over those with no invested interest or without recourse—changing nature's features for generations, it becomes a sell-out for the majority and a profit for a selected few. Politics dictate that there should be jobs and income for the populace. It's hard to argue against food on the table and a roof overhead. But those extracted resources are not unlimited, nor can they be replenished. Furthermore, the "boom to bust" mentality does little towards stability of families, income and advancement of opportunity for its residents. These industries not only rape the land, but the people as well.

Graceful in flight, the eagle does not fly—but soars. Mankind flies but rarely soars above his capabilities, though the possibilities exist and are limitless. We know we are so correct in our decisions regarding resource management that we believe our vision is shared by all other creatures. In nature there are penalties for man's foolishness. The conscientious individual would be wiser to borrow than to steal a resource.

Rope the wind—then let it go.

Cowboy Up

"Cowboy Up". Folks back East haven't the foggiest about some western terminology. And a lot of "Westerners" have forgotten their heritage. Unfortunately in both instances, it's the old scenario of the ignorant meeting the ignorant. One side never knew, and the other side has forgotten everything they learned. Life deals out some hard knocks. Like poker, one can either raise the ante, fold, or call. I've done all three at various times throughout my life. It's not what cards you're holding, but having a pretty good idea what the other fellow has in the way of a hand. If I could know for sure what the others had in their hands—hell, I'd win every game, or at least break even. But I can't read the back of the cards and the "Lucky Lady" isn't leaning over my shoulder either. So, one has to take chances, just like in life.

I've always believed that living life should be a pleasurable experience—like playing a good game of poker. If your goal is to constantly win, then you've already lost the game. Doing one's best is better than playing to win. After all, the road traveled has more importance than the destination. I'm going to get there, one way or the other—its how I get there that really matters.

When the cowboy gets bucked off a horse, a bull, or whatever critter is trying to do him in–it becomes a matter of pride when he pulls himself up, holds his head high, and limps out of the arena in the direction of his next ride. No matter the pain, the defeat, or personal loss he feels—he goes forth to take on his next challenge, and by doing so, shows everyone that he is up again—"Cowboy Up".

The day after Veteran's Day, I stopped in at the VA Center in Cheyenne to ask some questions of the civilians that worked there. What I encountered was long waiting periods and in general, a non-caring attitude. (For example, I was told that if I needed dental care I could make an appointment. The earliest I could see a dentist was July of next year.) That's your tax dollars at work–the same tax dollars that each person in the military pays as well. The individuals that I had conversations with that were caring had a sense of humor and that shared were—Veterans. Some were fighting for their lives, and edging their way through this bureaucratic nightmare with dignity. "Cowboy Up". This would be their last ride.

I next traveled to the main Post Office in Cheyenne. It's a nice, new government building—all the modern stuff. The employees that worked behind the counter were nice as well. But I had to stand in line fifteen minutes before I reached the counter. While standing in line I read the poster on the wall that said it was illegal to have firearms on postal property and that it was a felony offense. (One has to be caught first, of course.) After waiting in line for fifteen minutes and reading that poster, I think the employees were anxious of how I felt about government service in general.

My next stop was to the veteran's advisor at the Wyoming Job Center (which is not on Yellowstone highway anymore). Veterans helping veterans—right. There's something about the human mentality that I've never been able to overlook. It seems that when things are going well for the individual doing the listening, that the distance increases between the one explaining the problem and the one doing the listening. The playing field is not level at this point in time. People just don't pay attention nor do they care unless they have a personal stake involved—like poker. It's human nature.

But every now and then I do meet and talk with a person who honestly cares about other folks—willing to take a chance and stick his neck out for others; a person who has sand, and tells it like he sees it. Sometimes, he's been there too. Gorgeous George (alias, President Bush) has been rattling his saber for quite some time now about terrorism and more recently, Iraq. He's been giving Saddam ultimatums and has basically rattled the old boy's cage to the extent where the American public might even believe that Iraq poses a threat to us. Now, Gorgeous George is no fool—he knows where the oil comes from and Big Business and Big Brother are working hand in hand toward achieving a common goal—more money. (I just wish that Georgie Boy would finish the first job before starting another. Afghanistan is not over and already the agenda is on the table for the next go-around.) Meanwhile, "back at the ranch" the economy is still sucking wind, the environment is going to hell in a hand basket, we have a lame duck (some call it something different) Congress in session, the Democrats are wiping their tears (and other bodily regions), the Republicans are gloating (for now) about their victories, and the rest of America is trying to make ends meet. Our sons and daughters may once again pay the price, if they're in the military, and the Veterans are…well, just shaking their heads at what all has been lost along the way.

Putting all politics aside, one should ask the basic question: "Is your life any better in terms of quality than what it was a year ago?" If the answer is yes–then you're probably a Republican. If your answer is no–then you're probably human, and more in tune to actual events than what other people are.

He picks himself off the ground, aching back and sore muscles—something pops in his neck and his legs don't work in unison quite like they should. Bending over gently, he reaches for his smashed and dirt-covered Stetson with one arm extended to the ground. The floor of the arena dances dizzily in his vision and he is acutely aware of a throbbing pain in the back of his head, as his fingers encircle the crown of his hat—carefully he straightens to his recovered height. There is a loud ringing in both ears, so much so that he cannot hear the crowd that is standing in the bleachers—yelling something…he can't hear their roar or their applause. He angles his head towards the scoreboard to look at the final time…eight seconds!

He has made it…but doesn't see the clown's frantic actions, or the coming storm. The bull drills him from behind, knocking his body upward towards the rafters above…and towards those bright lights—such pretty lights, and one in particular…the brightest light whose intensity continues to grow, as he rises higher towards it. "Cowboy Up".

Cheyenne

Selling oneself is hard work at times. Throughout my travels in this state's capitol in search of employment opportunities, I have found most of the people that I have encountered to be courteous and busy with their own work schedules. I've also stumbled upon other facets of life in this "village".

Today, I took a little time for myself and visited a couple of places. I started the morning with a quick breakfast at Hardee's Restaurant around nine o'clock in the morning in which I discovered that this is a favorite time of the day for the elderly to meet and chat with each other, if only over a cup of coffee. Laughter, conversation and a friendly atmosphere prevailed.

After this amicable geriatric session, I headed downtown to the Wyoming State Museum and was greeted by a wonderfully nice elderly lady at the reception desk who explained the museum layout and the exhibit locations. Admission is free, as is the kindness of the staff. I viewed the history of the state from various perspectives and exhibits. Upstairs, I looked at the paintings, sculptures and sketches of different artists—none of which I found personally interesting. But, all in all, the museum was worth the visit.

I next traveled to the Cheyenne Frontier Days Old West Museum. (I'd visited in years previously, but I wanted to see it again.) Admission is five dollars, and for the first-timer it is worth it. The staff was friendly though busy preparing for an upcoming event in the building. If you're into wagons, carriages, cowboys and rodeo—then this is a good place to visit, though it's rather dead this time of year with no rodeo driving attendance. (I was the only one visiting at the time.)

When I visited this town thirty-four years ago the Cheyenne airport was at the edge of town, out in the countryside. Now, it's in the center of things. All day and night one hears aircraft from the airport and Francis E. Warren Air Force Base taking off and landing. These sounds are perhaps comforting to local residents, but triggers flashbacks in this old Army fuddy-duddy. I could live without the sounds of aircraft and automobile traffic outside this motel room. The Cheyenne Fuzz (police) are everywhere, looking for new prey. Seems they always have someone pulled over somewhere, especially at night. I haven't been pulled over yet because I've ignored them. Like a bad itch, I just hope they go away. I may start walking more, though.

For a city of fifty-three thousand plus, it's not a bad place (I've been in worse locations). The "Magic City of the Plains" still has some charm for this boy from the country. General Grenville Dodge of the Union Pacific Railroad established this tent city for the first transcontinental railroad and Army General C.C. Auger put together Fort D.A Russell to protect this new community back around 1867. The town was named after the Cheyenne Indians, who were thereafter disposed of in accordance with local customary manners. At 6,062 feet in elevation, the town is higher than its "mile-high" neighboring suburb, known as Denver. The air is also cleaner. (In Wyoming, any air pollution that we generate is generously disposed of on the wind currents towards the states back east. It's the native way).

Nothing comes close to a main event in this town as does the Cheyenne Frontier Days held the last full week in July. Although it is the state capitol and the legislature meets here over coffee and doughnuts at various times throughout the year, their rodeo is nothing compared to the town's rodeo of events during July of each year. The streets are packed with traffic, the town lights the town lamps at night, the drunks patrol the streets and keep the Fuzz in line, and the Cowboys are no longer a rare and forgotten sight. It's the "Marti Gouge of the West" where the merchants can make up their lacking bank accounts for the year with visitor dollars. But it's fun anyway. Everyone should see the rodeo and at least one night event.

Oh, I know that I'm probably being satirical in some of my views, but if Cheyenne wasn't worth the visit I wouldn't be here. There is still a flavor of the West here, though lacking somewhat in aroma. (I have yet to visit the Capitol Building, but doughnuts and politicians are strange bed fellows.) Having lived and breathed ranch life on several occasions north of this fine town, I do find it exhilarating to explore the city life.

This town is rich in history, populated by some of the finest examples of humanity I've had the pleasure to encounter, and is my hope for the future. I guess some things never change.

Cowboy's SOP

I am reminded of a time when everything that was "essential" for one's existence was stored in the rucksack and uncomfortably shouldered to wherever its owner was sent. This did not include one's weapon or other embellishments carried externally such as a knife, flashlight, burn packet, canteen(s), butt pack, compass or ear plug case. And no matter what the Standard Operating Procedure (SOP) said regarding how every item was to be properly stored in the rucksack, I inevitably had to dump out every damn thing in there to find what I was looking for.

I attribute this method of madness to the Army's sadistic humor and its continual search for ways to insure that what little sanity I had remaining would be swept away when everything "heated up" and I had more important things to worry about other than "organization". And while I have removed myself from those years of organizational chaos I still must consider at times what is essential and what is not.

Now that I am in the process of moving and not "deployment" I should rationally be able to do it the "civilian" way, which is to basically take what is needed and not required, open the tailgate of my truck, and throw all of it in the back without regard to placement or survivability. I should then be able to start the truck without any kind of maintenance checks whatsoever, (even if it is an operational risk—we used the term "Dead-Lined" in the Army) and steer towards my destination without regard to terrain, weather conditions, enemy drivers or leaving the line of departure on time. That's why we pay for automobile insurance. Might as well get your money's worth.

I don't have to do a deployment packet before leaving or update my personnel file to insure that my next-of-kin are correctly listed (that one really builds one's confidence prior to departure), nor do I have to do a detailed inventory list and put into storage non-military items that I can't take with me. I don't have to worry about my last will and testimony, shot records, my military I.D. card, or dog tags. Nope, I just climb in the old truck and haul ass, or anyone else's that wishes to go along on the trip. The only accountability I have is zip—it's the Cowboy way. The only SOP for communications is to turn my cell phone off (I can't hear it ring over the engine noise) and crank up my stereo with some good country music blaring away as I deftly maneuver through traffic jams and scenes of just-occurring automobile accidents. The fact that I may not make it to my destination is of no importance to me, until the truck quits, and that's when the cell phone gets turned on.

However, there are a few things that even the Cowboy must remember during his deployment exercise. First and foremost, one does not throw empty beer cans out the window when the cops are following (make sure the wind is right and that they land in the pickup's bed). Secondly, if one is pulled over by a "Law Dog", do not under any circumstances appear to reach for the rifle visible in the window gun rack (especially in Wyoming). Thirdly, quickly put on a seatbelt (it saves on ticket costs). And lastly, when looking at the officer through blood-shot eyes (disguised by dark sun glasses) and replying to his insistent questioning regarding one's evasive driving techniques, be sure that the breath mint in one's mouth does not hamper the slurred speech anymore than necessary.

All of the previously mentioned items may be rather difficult to remember, especially the order in which they occur. If asked to get out of the truck do so nat-urally–the officer will expect it anyway. Casually lean against the door of the truck (for stability) and portray the best "ah…shucks" personality one has. If nothing has worked up to this point, then the Cowboy will be told to turn around and to place his arms behind his back, wrists in waiting.

This is not a good time to request permission to finish the beer one has started or to further seek escape and evasion techniques. (Escape and Evasion Tech-niques come under a different chapter.) In due time, one will be standing before a magistrate of some sort. Similar to capture by the enemy while in the military, do not tell the magistrate any more than what he already knows (he already knows a lot by now anyway). Appear guilty in demeanor while maintaining the "good ol' boy" personality, and explain to the magistrate how after months of being bucked off horses, slammed into corrals by ornery steers, cut by barbed wire while mending fence, chaffed by seventy mile an hour winds while pitching hay, trampled by bulls during feeding, and having no time off to replenish one's depleted beverage supply—that there really is no excuse for the behavior one exhibited while driving and when pulled over by the officer.

If this is the first offense committed, then the magistrate just may let it go. If this is a second (or third, or fourth) offense then one should have read the chapter concerning "Escape and Evasion Techniques" prior to apprehension! That's the Cowboy's SOP.

Circumstances

Few things are worth doing if they're not done well. This week wraps up as a busy one for me personally. I started by moving into my apartment after hauling everything from Westminster, Colorado last Sunday. I was up by four o'clock in the morning and heading north up I-25 towards Cheyenne by 5:30 a.m. Of course, I didn't make Cheyenne until eight o'clock that morning because the snow was flying and the interstate was covered in ice, which probably attributed to the number of vehicles I spotted in the ditches along the way. I slowed down to forty-five miles an hour and still had problems keeping the rear of my truck back where it belonged.

Monday I went to work for a temporary employment agency and by this Saturday the company the agency had sent me out to work for had hired me full-time. Somewhere in between there was Thanksgiving day, which for me consisted of a day off from work and a enjoyable meal that I prepared all by myself—baloney sandwich, pretzels, carrots with ranch dressing, a Snickers candy bar, and a beer. (I'm a hell of a cook.) Now, that menu may not turn too many people's cranks but I was thankful anyway because I had something to eat and the day off. One needs only to drive along some of the main streets here in Cheyenne to see people less fortunate with their pack on their back, shuffling along looking for a meal or a lift to get them through one more day.

Circumstances, whatever they are, sometimes places one in less than desirable conditions. That fellow with the pack on his back is a human being too. It's just that he's cold and probably hungry, and doesn't know yet where he'll find a place to get out of the wind for the night. He's probably got a family out there somewhere, though circumstances have distanced them. "Bums" is the first thought entering most folks minds as they glance at them from inside their warm vehicle, never looking in their rear view mirror as they disappear with the increasing distance. Besides, "distance" protects us from the effects those people could have on us. We all have enough on our minds as it is and we shouldn't concern ourselves with the unfortunate ones who can't get their own life in order. (Very few people I know really have their life in order anyway.)

Throughout history there have always been those less fortunate. The reason I mention these things now is because…it's that time of year, folks! That's right– Thanksgiving is over with and it's time to start thinking about what you're going to get everyone and what everyone is going to get you. The Christmas sales are on, the bargains are waiting for your decision—and the merchants are waiting for your credit card (that's okay; you'll pay for it later!). Spend, spend, spend–shop till you drop time of the year. It's time to pay homage to others by getting them something (and vice versa).

My intention here is not to instill guilt. I know that family and friends are close. I know what it is to love someone who may not know or share similar feelings. But I also know what it is like to be treated kindly and with compassion by someone you've never met. "Gifts" are not always packaged with pretty paper and ribbons. Sometimes the most precious gifts are those never expected nor earned—circumstances.

Grandmother told me years ago that I could go anywhere and do anything because I was "adaptable". And I have adapted to a multitude of things, as I'm sure everyone has throughout their lives. I've always felt that it sometimes takes awhile for the bumpy road to finally get paved. I know that my road isn't paved yet and that I might not ever see a smooth highway but that shouldn't prevent one from traveling anyway.

This season I've decided that I'm going to do something special for someone that I don't know at all. Shortly before Christmas day I'll be traveling down one of these streets in Cheyenne and I'll see someone with a pack on their back, shuffling along a sidewalk on a cold and windy day, and I'm going to pull that beater truck of mine over to the curb. If that doesn't scare them, then I'm going to tell them to get in the truck if they want a warm meal in a restaurant somewhere (because I'm not really a hell of a cook) and we're both going to get a good meal inside a warm building out of the cold and the wind, and stuff ourselves. Then, I'll drive them to wherever they want to go in town. And who knows, I might even find out all about their…circumstances.

Guns and Ammo

Most people who own a gun don't know how to load it. That's not to say they don't know how to place a bullet in the chamber or to fire the weapon. More specifically, they don't know how to reload their own bullets. They buy everything pre-packaged and go out to the range or the nearest street corner and start firing away. Some folks I know are good marksmen and have decided to forego the reloading process. But the expert marksman reloads his own ammunition for accuracy. I've reloaded a variety of calibers but I don't consider myself an expert marksman. Though I do hit what I'm aiming at, whether using bullets or words. (Some targets don't enjoy that.)

Part of what is wrong with our society today in the way it views and uses firearms is that the foundation upon which our heritage and independence was founded has eroded away. Much like our evolution from horses to automobiles, nearly everyone drives something now. But not everyone can sit in a saddle and stay there without having an accident. Just like good drivers who have an accident, good horsemen have wrecks too.

When our country was in its infancy everyone had a rifle to put food on the table and to keep the enemy at a distance. It was a necessary tool, and later, a necessary weapon in gaining our country's independence. Everyone who owned a firearm reloaded. If one couldn't master the reloading process then the weapon could not fire. Simple. Of course, I'm talking about the age of black powder firearms. In loading a rifle the first thing was to insure it wasn't already loaded! We call that safety.

Powder was poured into a powder measure (not directly down the barrel) that was configured in "volume" of grains (unlike today's smokeless powder configured by weight) and the powder in the measure was then poured into the muzzle end of the barrel (thus the term "muzzleloader"). The side of the barrel was slapped by hand to insure the gun powder was deposited at the bottom of the barrel (breech end). Next, a patch or piece of patching material was laid over the muzzle end of the barrel and the (real) lead ball was placed centered with the tiny flat side of the ball (from the bullet molding process) facing upward. A ball starter was useful in starting the patch and ball down the barrel to the depth of four to six inches, and then the ramrod could be used to force the patch and ball down to the level of the powder inside the barrel. A finer grade of black powder (or primer) was then poured into the pan where the flintlock was located. (Technology later adapted the flintlock to the percussion firearm utilizing a small cap fitted on a nipple.) The hammer was pulled to the rear and locked until the trigger was pulled.

After firing some rounds, the shooter eventually had to clean the barrel to insure that the next patch and ball could be seated properly. Pistols worked in the same manner, though shorter in length of course. Black powder is corrosive and all firearms had to be cleaned and properly maintained to function correctly. As the years progressed, the muzzleloader gave way to percussion rifles and pistols, and later revolvers. The same principles applied to the revolvers leading up to the Civil War, and times thereafter. Instead of loading the powder and bullet through the barrel, powder was poured into the front of each cylinder chamber of the revolver. Depending on the type of revolver, packing material (such as cornmeal) was sometimes used to fill the gap above the powder in the length of each cylinder hole to increase accuracy, before the lead ball was pushed into each cylinder hole by a rammer mounted beneath the barrel of the revolver.

Grease was applied in front of each cylinder hole to prevent chain-fire when the weapon was fired. At the rear of each cylinder chamber there was a nipple that required a percussion cap to be fitted for each chamber. Revolvers were single action—which meant that the hammer had to be pulled to the rear each time before the trigger would allow the revolver to fire a shot. Smoke, grease, and flash burns on the hands were the occasion. And if one of the percussion caps didn't fall off inside and jam the rotating cylinder, one might possibly get all shots off in good order.

Moisture was death for flintlock type weapons, and affected percussion firearms to a lesser extent. Lead balls or bullets had to be cast over a fire requiring the lead to be hot enough to pour into a bullet mold. Lead burns the skin so gloves were recommended, and breathing lead fumes in the melting process was probably responsible for our Forefathers attitude towards the British.

If a man was angry at his neighbor and grabbed a unloaded black powder firearm intending to use it upon his would-be target, by the time he got the damn thing loaded he had probably forgot what he was mad about. (Keeping a black powder firearm loaded all of the time eventually corroded the barrel.)

Today, victims are easy prey to the gun-toting predator that lacks intelligence and desecrates our firearms heritage. And for some of our politicians, the idiot who commits such crimes becomes their poster child for denying the remainder of all law-abiding citizens their right to own and bear arms. If the American public is willing to forego its firearm heritage, then it must be willing to sacrifice its freedom as well.

Casper

I'm not what one would call a "Cat Guy", but Casper and Butterball have been a part of this family for years. Born of the same litter, these kittens came into our household when we were a military family living at Fort Knox, Kentucky. My daughter, Amanda, was seven years old then and my son Thomas was two years of age. The kittens were their first pets. Each had their individual characteristics and mannerisms—and their markings were completely different. Butterball with his orange-like color and bold attitude differed from Casper, who was more subtle and sneaky. Casper was white with a tinge of gray on top of his head, which was eventually replaced with all white through the early years of his life. As brothers, one cat could not leave without the other becoming curious as to his whereabouts.

In 1989 they made the journey to Gillette, Wyoming from Fort Knox in the backseat of the car, and at night when we stopped at a hotel in Chamberlain, South Dakota where no pets were allowed, we secretly escorted them to our hotel room and let them out of their cage to roam the room premises. After being cooped-up for such a long trip the cats were thankful for their brief freedom in that tiny room. They would spend another week or so in the Best Western Hotel annex when we arrived in Gillette and were searching for a home to rent. Eventually, everyone (including the cats) was settled into our home. We later moved into a mobile home and of course, Butterball and Casper joined us.

Amanda and Thomas continued throughout the years in the various schools—growing and evolving as youngsters do in their adolescent and teen years. The cats evolved too, and grew older with age and new methods of instilling their will upon their family. Cats have no "Master". They don't need a Master and don't want a Master. They just want to be cats. Independent, they take what they need from life and enjoy things that we as humans can't comprehend. They can't be trained—cats train humans instead.

The years continued onward. Amanda graduated from high school and started a new life on her own, eventually settling in Denver. Thomas, the cats, and I remained in Gillette. Life was somewhat hectic for us four guys. It was the Big Guys (Butterball and Casper) verses the Little Guys (Thomas and me) and we were under each other's feet during that time period. Thomas' high school graduation was just several months away and both of us would soon be leaving Wyoming—what about the cats? They're family, and you can't just give family away (although that notion might have some qualities to it).

Amanda was to the rescue. In one fell swoop, she "whisked" the whiskers right out of the house and moved them to Denver. The years continue to roll by and she moved to another part of the metro area, taking the fury felines to yet another new home. But, now the years are finally catching with the cats. Butterball develops diabetes and requires an insulin injection each morning. Casper continues to lose weight. These once robust curtain climbers from hell are sleeping more each day—lacking the energy that in previous years was boundless. Amanda mothers and maintains the health of both cats through repeated trips to the veterinarian's office and the incurring medical expenses—but love knows no boundaries.

Yesterday, after many years, and the eventual anguishing hours of pain, Casper was put to final rest. Butterball seems to understand that his brother is not returning home this time. Amanda and Mike continue to love and to comfort him, knowing that his time with them may be ending as well. If cats could talk, they could tell the life story of my children—from toddlers to adults, and all the happenings in those intervening years.

I'm sure that both brothers shared secrets about the escapades and shenanigans they were capable of exploiting throughout all of those years upon us. Odd, that now I can't remember any of the bad ones.

Expectations

I stopped in at Wendy's restaurant on East Pershing Boulevard the other night on the way home from work. When it was finally my turn at the counter I gave the girl my order. She asked me, "Will that be to go, or will you be eating in our dinning room?" I glanced over at the booths and tables. "Ah...I guess for here, please." (I was still trying to locate the "dinning room" in this fast-food joint.)

I reckon some folk's expectations are higher than mine. I just wanted something to eat and had no intentions of "dining" at Wendy's restaurant. If I was going to "dine" somewhere it would have to be a bit classier than at Wendy's. That got me to thinking about when was the last time I did any dinning. To me, dinning is being ushered to a table covered with a linen table cloth, with linen napkins, crystal glasses and expensive china, with real silverware and a waiter that wears a vest and a towel over his arm. Dining is spending more money on the tip than what a truck load of Whoppers cost. I've actually dined a few times in my life and found that the meal, although good, was overly expensive and not nearly large enough for my appetite.

I don't mind dressing up and going out to eat. A clean pair of Wrangler jeans, polished cow-kickers, pressed shirt with a good western pattern to it, and of course a brushed cowboy hat—all make me feel pretty good about eating out. If I have to wear a suit, tie and slacks…well, the fun of dining out has already started to bottom out. I really don't want to be like another Joe Smo, because I'm not. I don't make the money Joe Smo makes, and if I did, I wouldn't waste it like he does. "Dining" to me means going out and having a good meal with someone that enjoys the "atmosphere". Good dinner conversation and some two-stepping music after the meal—all in the same place.

This time of the year, there's the Christmas parties going on. People go out to "dine" somewhere the company has chosen for the year's event and where all the workers are told how much they are appreciated—and what a great year it has been for the company, and yak, yak, yak…Everyone feels they must go to these things just so their boss notices that they are indeed supportive of the company they work for. Everyone dresses up for the occasion, looking their best for the part. Everyone has to "mingle" so as to appear that they get along with everyone in the company. Tip a few drinks, slap a fellow or two on the back, and make a few jokes etc.—all in the holiday tradition. The company usually pays for the meal and the first few drinks. There might even be a live band for the event. But in the final analysis, the occasion is nothing more than a grand smorgasbord of assembly line food preparation and meals ready-to-eat. One can usually tell how well the evening is going by how many folks are stacked-up at the bar instead of being "captivated" by the company's schedule of events.

But, it's the holiday season so why not enjoy a free meal. (The company has made everyone suffer for the whole year so why not get a little something out of them in the end.) Nope, that's not for me. Now, if I was the boss and wanted to show my employees how much I appreciated their efforts for the year I would instead give them their choice of eating at a real "Dining" establishment that had a good menu, good live music, and a company tab. They could dress for the occasion instead of for the company, go dinning when they choose, and take that pretty little filly for a whirl on the dance floor after dinner without worrying about what kind of impression they'd be making on their fellow employees or the boss. And if that dining establishment had linen table clothes and napkins, real silverware and crystal glasses and a waiter that said "Ma'am" and "Sir" well, all the better.

And afterwards they could return home or to wherever, and say with all honesty, "Wow, I had a great time tonight!" The employee might even think that the old man wasn't such a lousy boss after all. Who knows, company productivity and inventiveness might even improve during the year that followed. Wendy's really isn't a bad place to eat—even their "dining room" is okay. Real folks eat there, with no pretensions. But if one has any expectations of having a good time they would be better off looking elsewhere.

And if the company thinks that they have guaranteed their survival for another year with employee loyalty after giving them a free meal then the company has forgotten the old adage–"There's no such thing as a free meal". You get what you pay for. If you want to have a good evening out—then one just has to make the effort.

Blown Away

I watched the truck driver back his eighteen-wheeler up to the dock. He then got out of his tractor and came on inside the warehouse. "Damn—the wind is blowing hard outside!" he exclaimed. "Yep, it sure is this morning. Where are you from, Sir?" I asked him. "I'm from Mississippi" he replied. "This is the first time I've ever been to Wyoming. Does the wind always blow like this here?" "Well, Sir…the wind usually blows all the time here. It's just a mite gusty this morning is all." "Does it ever not blow here in Wyoming? I mean, I was doing just fine in that rig of mine until I hit the Wyoming state line, then all hell broke loose!" "Well, once in a great while the wind stops blowing altogether," I replied. "It must be nice then without the wind blowing" he stated. "Actually, when the wind stops blowing here in Wyoming it's awful hard on the cattle." "How can the lack of wind be hard on the cattle?" the truck driver asked. "Well Sir, it's like this. You see the cattle are use to the wind blowing all of the time here in Wyoming, so they're always leaning into it. When the wind doesn't blow, the cattle just fall over and then they have a hell of a time getting up again."

I don't know if the young man believed me or not, but at least he had a story to take back with him to Mississippi. Eventually we had his truck unloaded and he was on his way to his next destination. We made a couple of deliveries in Cheyenne in the morning and then headed east on Interstate 80 for our next delivery in Sidney, Nebraska. The wind actually helped us in our truck going east and we reached 80 mph with no problem, until the governor kicked in and slowed us down. We took the Cabella's exit into Sidney and unloaded at the customer's home in town and started our return trip to Cheyenne.

Of course the wind was anything but helpful going west on the interstate. We flew our twelve-foot, two-inch high box kite home the best we could. Looking into the far horizon as the sun was setting; the light reflected the wind-whipped clouds with shades of crimson and pink hues.

I thought of the many years that had passed since my first arrival to Wyoming coming from this same direction and how expansive this country was then as it is now. Thirty miles east of Cheyenne my reflections were disrupted by the pungent smell of the refinery from the south of town whose odors were seeking out our senses. (That part I had no memory of so many years ago.) Since I live in that particular part of town I have occasionally thought about what would happen should that particular refinery decide to blow-up some day. I imagine that the resulting blast would be enough to take out my few apartment windows—even at ground level.

I live on "the other side of the tracks", which is to say…it's not prime real estate. But it's cheaper than other neighborhoods in town. I didn't pick the location for the scenery or the real estate—if I had, I probably wouldn't be living in Cheyenne anyway. (It's not the ranch, where the only night sounds are the wind and coyotes howling in the distance.) But, it's my home for the present so I make the best of it.

Anyway, I've figured out that I could be blown away in my apartment just as easily as on the interstate on a windy day, neither of which would be beneficial to my health. At least on the calm days in town, I'm not tripping over the fallen cattle.

Life's Little Pains

Every night when I finally arrive back at my apartment, something hurts somewhere. I don't know whether I am old, or just getting older. But the pain is somewhere because it lets me know it's there. Even if I don't feel pain I certainly feel tired. I head for a hot shower and steam up the bathroom mirror. I like doing that—steaming up the mirror. Makes me feel like I've accomplished something worthwhile.

Sometimes the hot water in the building goes on the fritz and I can't get it hot enough. Makes me want to throw my bar of soap at someone. Other times I get the water too hot and I end up jumping around in the shower like a scalded cat trying to dodge the water as I desperately try to find the handles to control the temperature before I turn into a lobster. I think that someone is plotting this water thing—like they know that when I get home at night the first thing I do is climb into the shower and…wham! "Got you again buddy…been waiting all day to get you when you got home!" (There are some sadistic folks out there.)

Indoor plumbing has been around for years now and you'd think we would have improved on it somehow. Computers have been around even less time and they're supposed to be high-tech machines. So this last Friday after a shower that I couldn't even steam the mirror with, I decided to add a Windows XP feature off the CD I had. Pop the CD into the tray and…wham! Everything locks up on the computer. So I shut the computer down and reboot again. I have the sounds in the background when it starts up but no desktop screen. Matter of fact–I don't even have a screen. Just blank.

So in my typical fashion I just go…blank. Now Windows 2000 and Windows XP systems are suppose to be really stable systems, unlike the other 9X programs (Windows 3.1, Windows 95, Windows 98 and Windows ME systems.) But I blew that theory for Dear Old Microsoft, thank you. I didn't go to bed Friday night because the remainder of the night was spent partitioning and formatting the hard drive, reinstalling all of my software programs, configuring the external devices, reestablishing internet connections, and downloading the updates from Microsoft, etc. I was in pain of a different category—mental. Fortunately, I've been down that road before so I only had to rely on my tired body to get me through the process again. By seven-thirty Saturday morning I had everything up and running again…but me.

I headed for the shower again with no better results than the previous evening. Now, I don't know who it is in this apartment building that is keeping tabs on my schedule but they sure have figured out this shower thing. I mean, how many times is someone going to attempt to foil my pleasure at steaming up a mirror?

Sunday morning when I arrived back at the apartment I bumped into the maintenance man and I showed him that there was moisture around the base of the toilet that was slightly seeping into the bathroom carpet. Now I know what that indicates–it means the wax seal between the toilet base and the floor needs replacing. (I've been down that road before too, but since I'm a tenant and not "responsible" for replacement, I let the maintenance man do his job. Isn't life grand!) Well, I get home from work this evening ready to make a go for my hot shower again. But the maintenance folks have been here today while I was gone. They replaced the wax seal and the carpeting. And left glue and other gunk on the porcelain around the toilet, in the bathtub, on the walls of the bathroom and the walls of the hallway, not to mention the dirt and debris on the carpeting from the bathroom to the front door. I've replaced wax seals between the toilet and floor before but I don't recall using a team of horses to do it.

I spent the next hour cleaning out the stables that I call my apartment. I know that the maintenance folks had good intentions and I should be more apprecia-tive but, gee wiz, I just wanted to steam up my mirror. I did purchase curtains for my apartment windows this weekend. Because I live below ground level (my life story) and I only had blinds in the windows it meant that every time someone pulled into the parking lot at night their headlights shot right through my blinds and I'd wake up to a laser light show. (Three-thirty in the morning and I thought a squadron of flying saucers had landed!) Now I can at least try to sleep in the dark. Except...for the hot water baseboard heating system. All night long the water lines are popping and cracking in the walls and I think somebody's out there shooting at me again. Or I wake up wanting to shout, "Grenade, Grenade, Grenade!"

This city life isn't all glamour for this country boy. Tomorrow, when I arrive here from another day's work I'll probably be in pain again. I'll want a steamy shower, and by eleven o'clock in the evening I'll want to get some sleep. But life's little pains will most likely interfere with that schedule of mine. So, I've decided to forego the schedule and do the unexpected. I'm going hunting for that sick psycho who keeps playing with the hot water.

Cowboys

"Are you a cowboy", the boy asked. "No son...I'm not a cowboy." "Well, you look like a real cowboy to me. How come you're not a cowboy?" I looked down at the little boy from atop my horse and thought about my answer before replying. "Well, son...all the real cowboys are gone."

All the cowboys are gone...Though, there's still a lot of "Want-to-bee's" around these parts. From head to foot–the cowboy was a working man. A good felt hat with a brim for any kind of weather–not some baseball cap or hat made from straw. He wore a bandana around the neck instead of the tie that the bean-counter wears. A long sleeve flannel shirt with the top buttoned. Cotton duck coat instead of some synthetic material with pretty colors that spooks a horse. Good one-piece leather belt around the waist with leather gloves, chaps and leather boots with a good heel for the stirrups—not tennis shoes or clod-hoppers that the walking stiff wears. There weren't any fat cowboys. Fat "cowboys" or those with a good gut couldn't ride a horse. They weren't much good for anything else either.

Real cowboys know how to rope, ride a horse and drink whisky straight. They know when to get drunk, but aren't dependent upon their liquor to see them through the day. Cowboys aren't braggarts, but are soft spoken men who can recognize an arrogant, loud-mouthed, opinionated ass at first glance, but they have manners enough to keep their mouth shut anyway. They do the best job they are capable of and when the boss is wrong—they move on.

There's a difference between a cowboy and a ranch hand. A ranch hand is a laborer without pride. A cowboy rides for the brand. A ranch hand works for his paycheck while the cowboy works because it's his specialty. Cowboys enjoy an occasional smoke of good tobacco and don't need pot, drugs or a cigarette every fifteen minutes to make it through the day. And they don't expound upon proper riding techniques or saddle and tack knowledge that may have been obtained from some literary source, because they know every horse is different—just like humans. And they sure as hell don't drive their horse into the ground because they feel like it. Cowboys draw the cinch tight because roping from a loose saddle is an invitation to disaster. They work from their horse. And when they get a run-of-the-mill mount that everyone else has ridden they know it's only a matter of time before the horse explodes under pressure.

Good horses, like good cowboys, are a specialty. A cowboy never walks when he can ride. Cowboys don't ride for the sport or a buckle. There's a lot of talented rodeo stars but few real cowboys that ride the rodeo. They call themselves "athletes" nowadays. They've got all the glitter and commercialism they can attach to their exteriors, but still lack the "heart" of the west. A cowboy carried guns—usually a revolver and a rifle. Weapons were necessary tools on the frontier. They drank coffee for breakfast—not some kind of soda pops, and appreciated every good meal because their strength and stamina depended upon eating.

But the most identifying characteristic of the real cowboy was that he loved the land and the way of life he lived upon that land. The wind in the grass…and a song in his heart.

"Where did all the cowboys go?" asked the boy. "Son, they left for the wide open spaces where's there's no fences" I replied. "They left a long time ago."

I turned my horse's head, and ambled on down that long road of years gone by. And I listened to the wind in the grass…and the song in my heart, following the tracks of those before me.

Kinships

In the upper portion of New York State, nestled beneath the Adirondack Mountains, a young country girl began her journey in life. I've never been to that geographical location, but folks tell me that it is beautiful there. A certain quaintness and solitude that builds character in a person.

I never knew the young girl then, but I was fortunate to have met her years later. She and her family lived just a couple of doors down from our military quarters and our children played together. As neighbors, in sometimes troubling moments, each knew that the other's home would always be a refuge to the other. Those were good times indeed. We had lots of get-togethers—cookouts, card games, even fishing and camp-outs on the lake. I can't remember who had the most fun—the kids or the adults.

Army life is hard on a soldier's family, sometime harder than it is on the soldier. A soldier takes orders and moves out. The family stays behind and supports each other and other families as well. What the civilian world sometimes forgets is that when you lose the soldier you lose the military family and their way of life. Few communities are as close-knit as the military community. And few friendships are as genuine as military neighbors.

In 1989 I departed from that particular military neighbor and said farewell to that young woman and her family. I've not seen her since then. But through the years we've somehow remained in touch with each other. Her life took a few drastic turns, eventually for the better, and my life…well; it took a few drastic turns too. It's comforting to see in pictures, letters and email how people's lives take on new meaning. Prideful mother of her children, and the wife of husband, the soldier. And through it all…a good, warm and caring person.

There are priorities in life. There are one-night-stands, acquaintances, friends, and kinship. I list these from lower to higher in priority (though some may disagree). One-night-stands are the easiest to forget (afterwards). With acquaintances you may recall the face but not the name (almost like one-night-stands). Friendships can be brief—or last a lifetime. But kinships are forever.

When I sit down to write I often think about the individuals who will first see my effort. Most are friends, and some are kinships. None are acquaintances. (Sorry guys and gals, no one-night-stands either.) What means the most to any individual is how well they are perceived by those who mean the most to them. What do I care if some jerk wants to get belligerent or go a few rounds with me. What my children or friends think of me is more important than some smuck whose character I've smudged. What few quality friends I do have means more to me than a bushel of attributes.

A "friend" has been defined as one who knows everything about you…and likes you anyway (or is too modest to tell you otherwise). Kinships evolve from friendships. What a wonderful way to begin.

Anyway, back to my story (and it's my story, so I can tell it anyway I want to). Today I received in the mail a card and a picture of this young lady with her husband and their sons. Her husband was home (fortunately) for Christmas when the picture was taken. I won't mention names because I believe in respecting the privacy of others (unless I have an axe to grind). But I do believe in sharing my thoughts regarding others whom have touched my life. And this particular lady has touched my life.

Years ago she shared her childhood stories with me of growing up in the countryside of New York State, things she did as a teenager, how much she loved and admired her father and the multitude of things he was capable of doing. She spoke of her children, her friends and her life as an Army wife. Her rich and vivid descriptions of the rustic landscape of upper New York State captured my imagination. And through each of the words spoken one could see what deep meaning this had in her life. And I tell you this story now because I am like an elephant (though smaller in size). I have a memory that lasts a lifetime. And the thoughts, words and deeds of others seem to stick to my feeble mind like flypaper at times. But always, it is the happier times and those that mean the most to me that stick the best.

When you're having one of those days where everything has gone to hell in a handbag like I had today, it's comforting to fall back on memories of good times. Kinships will always outdistance Distance. It doesn't matter where you are in the world or what you are doing at the moment. It matters little what your present frame of mind is at the time. Good days or bad ones are trivia compared to kinship.

Memories are like yesterday. "Tomorrows" are reminders of fleeting times. And all those microscopic bits of entity sometimes come together and gel into something more worthwhile than the bits themselves. From friendship to kinship...I salute that little lady...and thank her for just being there.

Simple Things

I enjoy the simple things in life. Like a good cup of coffee, home-made bread, bacon and baked beans. A warm, dry building when there's a cold snow letting loose outside. Frost on tree branches in early morning just as the sun breaks the eastern horizon and a slight breeze that reddens the face but warms the heart.

A good horse that nuzzles your back as you close the last gate for the day. The Meadowlark's song. I enjoy watching eagles soar overhead on the wind currents, or looking into the quiet somber eyes of a calf that is not spooked by my presence. Simple things that are perhaps beneath the dignity of the typical individual.

I don't need to watch television unless I wish to become depressed in due time by the advertisements portraying what everyone should buy in order to be happy. (Back in time before there was television there must have been a lot of miserable folks around.) I can't handle sitcoms. I enjoy meeting individuals that are courteous and who can engage in an intelligent conversation about themselves and the world as they view it. I'll take an objective person over an obnoxious, opinionated, loud-mouthed, know-nothing any day.

Fixing something that's busted up is more worthy than buying everything new, though there comes a time when some things are just plum worn out. (Sometimes I'm plum worn out and I worry about being replaced by something newer.) Simple things mean more to me than extravagance. I understand a lady's desire to wear ear rings for example. But for the life of me I can't understand why a "man" would want to wear them. And why stick one in your nose (or other places)? A tattoo can be okay for some folks, but why paint your body like a billboard? I don't understand orange and green hair but I can comprehend a man's bald spot. Besides, how much hair or what color it is doesn't tell anyone about the person inside. If you want to know about the person inside look into their eyes. If there's nothing in their eyes then there's probably nothing on the other side either. And if the wind whistles through their ears–you've got all the confirmation you need.

Simple things mean more to me than well-rehearsed oratory. I'd rather see it than have it explained to me. I'd rather feel it than read about it. I enjoy a good book but I'd rather enjoy a good person instead. (They don't have to be simple.) Wearing long johns on a cold winter day seems simple to me—going without them is a major ordeal here in Wyoming. (Changing in and out of them two or three times a day during the fall season is not, however, simple.)

Complicated individuals like simple things. Simple people make things complicated. I've met a few simple folks in my lifetime who complicated life for me in general, but who had good intentions. And I've met some individuals who were complicated that I've could have "fixed" with a simple solution. I've come to the realization that the more human nature strives to make life easier and simpler—the more complicated things become.

Eventually, technology will replace all of the menial things we do on a daily basis. There's gadgets and hi-tech stuff flooding the consumer market every day now, and if they break you don't have to fix them—just throw them away and get a newer version. I know some who complain about getting up in the morning and going to work at the same old job every day. Not me, though. (I may not know what the day has in store for me, but waking up alive is simple enough for me.) Besides, it's the only day I have. Yesterday's gone…and tomorrow isn't here yet. Simple things in complicated times–life's blessings.

Universal State of Mind

If individuals would use their talents for the good of mankind instead of their creative destructiveness what a better place this universe would be. For instance, last weekend some computer geek decided to let loose another variation of a worm virus that played havoc with some severs handling email and banking transactions. Of course, my email was affected because every deviate who wants to make a point attacks Microsoft software first. My banking transactions were not, however affected—because I have no money (can't get something from nothing). If this particular geek had used these talents towards the positive I'm sure that something more worthwhile could be accomplished instead of this vented destructiveness.

This sphere we call home travels throughout the universe yet mankind is determined to remain in the age of Neanderthal. I mean, how low do we have to become to where we have no mentality left at all? I've always enjoyed flying–it's so wonderful up there. The earth looks so peaceful, all the way to its curved horizons. (The clouds are so easy to step out unto and bounce lightly upon.) And the sun shines brighter—and if one is flying fast enough eastward, the night is only a few hours long. Certain visions will always remain in my mind—crossing the Pacific and Atlantic oceans, seeing from the air the Alaskan wilderness composed of mountains, snow and forests, the western plain states that seem to contain nothing but vastness, flying into a swirling storm front exceeding thirty-thousand feet in height with lightening all around. Turbulence that drops you several hundred feet in a matter of seconds, or that raises you upward so quickly that your stomach remains somewhere anchored near your feet. I've always been delighted at take-offs and landings that require a sharp bank and slide through the atmosphere where I can lay on my side looking at the ground at extended wing tip.

Having flown in helicopters as well brings out an even more unique aerial experience. Choppers can do things fixed-wing aircraft can't—and they can do it in a tighter fashion. They're not as fast as an airplane but when flying nap-of-the-earth you wouldn't know it because you're too busy concentrating on the next tree line or hill top hoping that there's enough clearance to make it over.

I went down in a chopper once when the engine oil pressure failed. But anytime you can walk off an aircraft after impact I consider it a good landing–and I'm still around. When I found out that my son Thomas had parachuted out of perfectly good airplane for the first time, I asked him how he felt. He explained that the hardest part was going out that door. I've gone out some doors in my lifetime and had them slam behind me. It's hard getting back in—and impossible if you're falling at over a hundred miles an hour going the opposite direction. He had a good landing, and had more fun doing it.

Okay, I'll take my wings off now and get back to this universe thing. Checking the various statistics regarding who views my website I am sometimes amazed at the audience. I don't know who the particular individuals are who find their way to my home turf but I can tell the type of computer software they are using, where they are located, whether it is thru the internet or commercial/military use, etc. For example, presently ninety percent of the users that are accessing my website do so through the internet and the remaining ten percent are commercial and military users. The majority users are in the Cheyenne area, but others are located throughout Wyoming, the United States, Mexico, Italy and the Netherlands, for instance. And the number of those accessing my website throughout the world continues to climb. I'm not sure what they're looking for or if they find it by dropping in for a visit, but there must be something turning their inquisitive cranks.

I'm no computer geek and seek no audience. I figure that the website is there for anyone to view and if anyone gains anything from it then that's enough for me. I try to maintain a positive, if not creative, perspective on things when I fiddle with my web pages. Hell, I'm just a country boy living in the upscale village of Cheyenne doing what most folks do on a daily basis—which for me is to eat, sleep and work for the most part.

But some individuals have more time on their hands I reckon, which is why they can come up with personal devilishness that impact upon a lot of individual lives. Like the morons that screw up the computer systems of others. The more advances we are capable of generating in bettering our lives and the lives of others the more determined a small segment becomes in creating havoc for others. These individuals are intelligent and capable of mighty deeds that could benefit others but instead use their efforts in undermining society. I don't know that they seek recognition or self-assurance but one thing I do know and it is this: the universe is far greater than their moronic mind. They should first learn to fly—and later soar.

Free Spirit

I long for the mountains again. I reckon that city life is for the city folks, and I don't count myself as one. But the mountains are not a favorable habitat for this ol' boy in the winter time. The trails through the passes fill up with snow and the glaciers grow this time of year. There are no open waters that shimmer as they do on a summer day.

Perhaps winter is becoming too long while the warm breezes of spring are still on a distant horizon somewhere. February of every year begins changes. The New Year is already underway—the holidays are over. Valentine's Day is coming up and I don't have a valentine or someone to send it to. So I completed my federal income taxes instead and sent them off last weekend. At least I'll receive a refund (without the usual interest that the government could have paid me while they used my money this last year). Gas prices at the pumps are climbing again as they usually do whenever the oil companies have reason to gouge the consumer. If the prices do go down it will only be if Georgie stops beating his drum. (Of course, the prices will be up there in time for the beginning of the summer tourist season).

The shoddiness of the major retailers such as Wal-Mart continues to be a burr under my saddle blanket. I shopped at Wally World last weekend and within four days the one loaf of bread I bought had gone moldy and the one gallon of milk that I had also purchased started to freeze up in the refrigerator. Guess there was too much water in both of them. The only place there is not enough moisture seems to be in the weather around here.

My daughter's Chevy truck four-wheel drive went out so she did the smart thing and got rid of it. General Motors wanted eight-hundred bucks to replace the motor in the transfer case so I agreed with her that she should look for another vehicle. No since throwing good money away. She bought a 2003 Honda and traded in the truck. Only problem is that she has to learn how to drive all over again. The new car has a manual transmission and somewhere in raising my son and daughter—I forgot to train her on a manual transmission. But she'll get the hang of it, if she doesn't wreck it in the process. (I told her to be sure and contact her insurance company for the new car coverage.)

The brain-dead drivers have taken control of the streets here in town once more. Last week somebody plowed into an electrical pole on Dell Range Boulevard and took out half the power in Cheyenne. Needless to say that included a lot of the traffic signals at the intersections. I don't understand why drivers are required to have driver's licenses to drive vehicles. When there are no traffic signals working at intersections that must mean that there are no traffic laws—right? I saw people barreling down the streets at forty miles an hour right through the intersections without yielding a right-of-way. (I also heard the sirens going for most of the morning as the meat wagons made their rounds to the various crash scenes.) Whatever happened to common courtesy? I have a new car and I'd like to keep it that way. I don't need some forty mile-an-hour idiot plowing into me when I'm stopped at an intersection that has a non-working traffic signal. Besides I'm "packing"–which for the layman means, I'm carrying a loaded concealed firearm (legally) and I don't want to use it in a confrontation with an idiot (however beneficial it may be to society). Come on folks, drive safely!

I started Monday of this last week by wrenching my back going downstairs into the basement with a four-hundred pound sofa sleeper at a customer's home. But I weathered the week with medication, more physical work, and beer. (I'm not sure that the medication and physical work helped any.) Fortunately, I haven't been sick or had a cold this season. I do have a cold medicine remedy that apparently works well for me though. If I do get sick I take two aspirins and a shot of whisky every half hour. No, it doesn't do anything for one's cold…but after awhile you don't care!

At least I'm still living up to the New Year's resolutions that I made to myself…which was not to make any resolutions. It's great to be a free spirit!

Too Much

I was at two of the Sam's Club stores in Louisville and Thornton, Colorado last week taking down and setting up displays. This process required going from the receiving dock, through the grocery areas, and onward to the center of the floor area. I had ample opportunity while negotiating back and forth through the crowd to view individual customer shopping habits. At first I was amazed at the quantity of food items in the carts. I had never seen so many items, even in grocery stores! Customers literally had stacks of food items in carts and on flatbed dollies that they were toting around through the store. Most had more food than I could consume by myself if I had an appetite that lasted six months or more. They had meat, milk, vegetables, and frozen foods in abundance.

The irony of this was not the quantity of foodstuff, but the individual consumer's appearance. In almost ever instance the shopper was not only overweight, but exceedingly fat. They leaned upon their carts and dollies, huffing and shuffling as they made their way through the grocery isles as if this effort required every bit of their exertion. Apparently, gluttony was in fine form this day. For some folks being overweight is a genetic thing. However, most who are overweight got into that condition with no small effort. They obviously had to eat (a lot) and maintain little (if any) physical effort.

As Americans, we present quite the picture to the outside world. Instead of remaining in the city proper and renovating or building a new home, we decide that five acres in a housing addition on the outskirts of town would be a better location for a new home. The fact that the land was once used for grazing or other agricultural purposes is of little concern. And like most new homes on the market that sell anywhere from a quarter of a million dollars on up, the home-owner has little regard for what others might think of this urban sprawl. Americans are the richest people in the world. Americans also consume a good majority of all of the natural resources as well.

Watching this week's news coverage of particular events primarily concerning Iraq, the United Nations, and the demonstrations against war throughout the international community reinforced the prevailing thought I have always maintained; that the rest of the world is getting pretty tired of America in general. And who can argue their right to feel that way. I've lived in Europe and I will readily testify that the international news coverage portraying the United States is not always favorable. The same story is broadcasted in an entirely different light here in the United States—making us better than we are really perceived worldwide.

Another news story that caught my attention was the one asking Americans if they felt that they were contributing to terrorist activities by driving their huge, gas-guzzling SUV's and furthering our dependence on oil. Survey says: No! Reality says: Yes! It doesn't take an Einstein to figure out that America's weakest link is its gluttony. Thinking back to the playground days of youth, any child could figure out that if there was one bully on the playground who made up all of the rules and took what he wanted whenever he desired, then it was just a matter of time until all the kids took care of that one bully. And if you think for one moment that our almighty dollar will protect us against the international community anytime we want to set the rules or to further consume resources meant for other nations and their people–you'd better think again.

I am, of course, playing the devil's advocate here. I love this country and its people–and I would die for both. Granted, we shouldn't have to worry what others may think of us. But we better do so, because though America is the most generous nation in the world, we are perceived as that bully on the playground. And if enough of the other kids get together, all that is too much—will become too little.

Liberty and Speech

One of the greatest liberties we have is that of speech. Sometimes that particular liberty gets me in trouble with some folks when I "expound" on some subject I have selected as a topic and that has piqued my interest. A recent comment directed to me from one dear friend suggested that, "There have been only a few that I thought you were a little preachy, but it was the opinion of the author and I read it as such". Honesty is what I desire from others and what I wish to offer in return. I appreciate comments such as the one given.

And while speech remains an inherent liberty and given right to all Americans, the subtle erosion of that particular liberty progresses unnoticed in many instances. I write what I feel and believe in my mind to be the truth, knowing that in doing so I will antagonize and distance some who do not see things in the same light. As a young boy reading the newspaper, my attention was always drawn to the top of the front page where posted was the quotation by Voltaire—"I disapprove of what you say, but I will defend to the death your right to say it". I don't know if that particular newspaper still carries that quotation on its front page, but I still carry it in my heart. And I believe strongly that its guidance applies in our time as well.

When individuals become so defensive in their attitude towards anyone offering a perspective that differs from their own, they in essence join the millions of other silent victims who speak not, and who create their own personal anxiety towards the individual offering that perspective. Rather than offer their own viewpoint in open debate they instead unsheathe a dagger intending to ruin the bold perpetrator of speech. In doing so, they extinguish the light of liberty for all. Subtle erosion of liberty created by deranged minds. I still recall the era of the "Silent Majority". Of course, that was part of the political agenda then. Politics and religion I've been told are two subjects not to be discussed between friends, less they become enemies.

Now, politics I don't mind discussing. All rational people, regardless of party affiliation, probably know that all politicians are crooked—otherwise they wouldn't be in the business of politics. Religion, on the other hand, I stay away from. What you personally believe in is your business and you alone answer to the Almighty–and believe me, I'm not getting in the middle of that relationship!

And so, at the risk of becoming "preachy" I offer my opinions to the public in the glaring light of liberty and freedom of speech, not to incite, but rather to further the processes of thought and discussion, always vigilant of the hidden dagger directed towards my backside. My father's favorite antidote towards unkind cuts was…"If you can't say anything nice, don't say anything at all!" And while I know that words once spoken can never be taken back, I also know that words never spoken (or written) cannot convey the thoughts and feelings of those who have so much to offer to others.

There are times that some things become too important not to share with others. Rather than keep these thoughts to myself hidden away in the innermost regions of my mind, I send them forth as Knights on a Crusade. Their purpose is the same—to shed light on topics overlooked in our daily lives, but still maintained in our subconscious minds. And perhaps along the way we discover who we really are, in the process of sharing ourselves with others.

Winter's Breath

Night stars sharply piercing the open pockets of blackened clouds of darkness and stinging cuts of cold seeking passage inside the folds of bundled clothing. There is no warmth here. Eyes tearing from winter's breath—how many seasons now has it been? Over half a century and yet one continues to endure.

Muscles stinging from tightness for what seems eternity. Paradise is an illusion of the mind and this, a mirage of nothingness. Only the mind can bridge the distance between nature and one's soul. Swirling snow settling as a comforter and blanketing this prone form imperceptible between ground and sky. The darkest of night just before the morning light. He had touched ground in the first hours of darkness and after ascertaining his bearings had slowly crawled to this location.

Even in the darkness the route seemed familiar. It mattered little that the other's life would end in daylight leaving himself susceptible in his escape. This was personal, and therefore worth the risk. How many times this same scenario? The eastern horizon flared minutely showing the beginnings of dawn. Slowly, he uncovered the weapon that lay beside him. Carefully adjusting the bipod at the end of the forearm so as to conform the rifle to the ground at shoulder height, and gently removing both lens covers on the scope. Positioned where the morning sun would be oblique to his position and incapable of reflection, he sighted through the scope's reticle to the corner of the building and did a quick estimation of four-hundred and seventy-five yards. He checked the distance three more times.

Urges of hunger and thirst were briefly dispatched in this depression of the earth—the cold was of more urgency now, and waiting for light. A muffled click as the bolt was pulled to the rear and a round inserted into the chamber. With a metallic whisper the bolt was closed and locked downward in one easy motion. A western breeze foretold of dawn's arrival. That was good—a breeze from the west would keep his scent away from the dogs that would surely become suspicious and might even indicate the general location where he lay. No motion, no sound, no scent. The minutes clicked by slowly—an hour passed and the sun crested the hills to the east, frost twinkling on the grassy stems.

First one figure, then another appeared walking among the buildings below. Their morning routine was well known to him. Only a matter of seconds and his target would appear. Silently he released the rifle's safety while sighting through the scope at the doorway of this one particular building. Breathe in, hold it, and slowly breathe out. Again, breathe in, hold it, and slowly breathe out...Finger caressing the trigger as a gentle lover in death. Breathe in, hold it, slowly breathe out...

He was wearing a red plaid coat when he stepped outside. Brisk and beautiful, this was a gorgeous morning to lift one's spirits. Already the air was beginning to warm in the morning light and spring was but a few weeks away. A roaring crack from the southeast halted his next step. He looked upwards toward the shadowy hills where the sound originated and waited as the echo reverberated down the valley. Silence engulfed him. And then...nothing, but the first trickle of snow melting from the branches overhead and splattering onto the snow at his feet.

The earth tilted, and the sun dropped behind the hills to the west. The first star appeared on the eastern horizon and a subtle breeze began the night's routine of dusky overture. The darkness ushered forth the cold once again as an old friend. Hours passed, and the lights in the valley below flickered out one by one. Another hour passed and a shadow lifted from the ground in the hills above the valley, and crept slowly up towards the dark ridge line.

Carefully examining the ground at his feet, the man bent over and lifted the rifle, engaged the safety lever, folded the bipod, and slung it over his shoulder. Reaching down, he clasped an arm and leg and lifted the heavy body over his shoulder and proceeded back down the ridge stopping briefly to retrieve his own rifle and gear. The return trail would be brutal but not nearly as murderous as it had been the other direction.

Snow began to fall and secreted this toil of travesty. One still living...the other one's life extinguished forever, this mission was completed. Just like the earlier days of his youth. Muscles stinging from tightness and eyes tearing from...winter's breath.

Dead Horse

No sense in kicking a dead horse. That's what I feel like–a dead horse. I've had this cold now for two weeks and even though it appears that it is now on the wane (I try to remain optimistic) I still suffer some effects. Everyone I've had contact with has cold symptoms of some degree. This, coupled with the change of jobs and the differences in my daily schedule, makes me feel like I've been drugged through a key-hole backwards. I don't sleep like I should, don't eat like I should, and basically don't do anything like I should. Actually, I don't feel like doing anything. I haven't felt so out of sorts since I was eighteen. I've lost weight (and I didn't have any weight to begin with) and physical energy.

Getting back to my apartment after work at six o'clock this morning I was faced with another task—laundry. I finished that by seven-thirty and hit the sack, only to keep myself awake with this irritating cough that only occurs when I'm just about to dose off. So I'm back up again by 10:30 a.m. and out the door to run some errands, grab a quick bite at Burger King and stop at Walgreen's for re-supply of cold medicine and vitamins. I've felt so lousy this past week that my beer supply has remained untouched. That's pitiful. Actually, I didn't want to mix alcohol with the cold medicine for fear of what I might really turn into.

The past week has been like a bad dream with the lack of rest, my daily schedule which has me out the door at six-fifteen in the evening and gone until six o'clock the following morning, trying to get to bed by seven in the morning, back up again by two in the afternoon, and out the door at six-fifteen again in the evening. The first morning after working all night I tried sleeping only to have the phone ring at nine-thirty in the morning. Telemarketers start their day early. Unfortunately, that particular telemarketer's day went to hell after I answered the phone. (I now turn the phones off in the morning.)

I've come to the realization that folks who work nights are not normal. (Yea I know, most folks who know me say that I'm not normal anyway.) The world evolves around those who work during the day and who sleep at night. Everything that "normal" folks do on a daily schedule is based upon a work-days/sleep-nights schedule. The folks that I work with at night invited me to breakfast at the Village Inn restaurant at the completion of work this morning, which I graciously declined. I told them I would have breakfast with them the next time. (That's one of my many downfalls—I just don't take a time-out and enjoy some of the little things in life—even if I did feel lousy at the time).

What I really need is someone to look after me. Oh, I can handle the everyday things such as work and sleep...work and sleep...but it's the little things in between that I'm deficient in. Like cooking for example. I can make a mean peanut butter sandwich and heat a can of soup with the best of them. (Some would say that my diet is lacking.) But that doesn't come anywhere close to making one a gourmet chef. That "someone" would also be a physician as well. "Gee wiz–you're looking a little frail. You need some mending and I'll get to working on you right away!" Or if I've had a bad day, that "someone" could psychoanalyze me and get my mind back where it belongs (and out of the gutter).

I've always known that the "perfect" job is one where they pay you to stay home. (My father's advice towards marriage was to "marry for money—you can always learn to love them later"). So in looking at those few necessary qualifications in becoming that special "someone" they would as a minimum have to be a cook, a doctor, a shrink, a mother, and wealthy.

I believe I have a better chance as a dead horse.

Baseball

We often forget just how much influence we have on younger people, such as children for example. As parents or grandparents we strive to set the example and to pass on our "lessons of life" to the younger generation, just as our parents and grandparents did for us. After all, when you were young you were immortal, and needed the guidance and wisdom of the old fogies to insure survival in your later years. Now that we're the old fogies and have genetically inherited the same parental genes, we readily pass on to the younger generation our own guidance and wisdom. Doesn't matter that they don't want or need our advice—we're going to give it to them anyway. Sometimes good intentions or the carelessly offered remark can have a major impact on a kid.

When I was still a tadpole all I could dream about was baseball. I collected and traded baseball cards, attended baseball games, and even played in the town's local little league. Each of the teams was representative of a major or minor league team. I played short-stop and left field on the New York Yankee's team in that little league. When I wasn't actually on the ball field in town I was back at the farm throwing tennis balls as hard as I could against the cement wall of the garage and fielding the "hits" as they came my way. Our team even had a picture in the local newspaper—all dressed in the Yankee's uniform. All of us sharp and good looking lads—and a winning team too! I still have the picture tucked away in the old army foot locker that I gave to my daughter.

One day while I was catching the "hits" off the garage wall I mentioned to my father that when I grew up wanted to play as a professional baseball player—in the big leagues. Yes, that was my goal and I knew that I was a good enough player to achieve that goal. I loved the game—the smack of the ball in the old glove, the crack of the bat, running down the base line, catching a line drive or a fly ball, the crowds cheering in the background…what a life that would be! Dad stated that I was a little to old to start thinking about that now and that I should have begun earlier if I wanted a career in baseball—other kids who had begun playing earlier in life would always have the advantage and possess more talent because of their experience.

By the end of summer my baseball days had ended—and my dreams as a ball player ceased to exit. I believed in my father's advice. After all, he was my dad and his words meant more to me than advice from anyone else. If you can't trust your parents who can you trust? But I was heartbroken anyway. He was right of course—all parents are. Besides, I had work to do on the farm, school to attend; homework to be done each evening...and fall was in the air. The World Series just didn't have quite the meaning it once had for me. If I wasn't good enough to play the game I saw little need to watch it as a spectator. I wasn't tall enough for a basketball career, though I played on the school team. I wasn't big enough to play on the school football team, and my parents wouldn't allow it anyway because of possible injury and the resulting doctor bills. So I would just have to pursue something else in life.

There was a guy with a white hat carrying a tray, standing in the isles yelling "Peanuts, Hot Dogs, Coke-Cola, Beer..." a cool and clear night with the bright lights of the stadium shining down on the field below. The bases are loaded and it's the bottom of the ninth inning with two outs...our own Indianapolis Indians are behind in the scoring. But tonight is a special night indeed. The Tribe has a guest manager on the team—none other than Ted Williams himself. And he puts himself into the line-up as the next batter.

The home crowd roars with approval and everyone is standing in the stadium. Ted Williams steps up to the plate—the pitcher winds up and cuts loose with a deadly fast ball. A swing and...the crack of the bat and the ball soars up...and up...out over the outfield wall. Ted Williams has hit a Grand Slam...and the Indianapolis Indians win the game!

What a night—what a great night! I got to see Ted Williams in person and watch him hit a grand slam home run. And I got to see all of it because of the man next to me.

You see, it was Father/Son night there in that stadium. All the boys and their fathers were there to witness what I had just seen. And I got to see it all...because my dad was right there beside me. Words sometimes hurt. But...action speaks louder than words.

War

I have the feeling of being led down a path that I don't want to travel. Like a subtle sleeplessness that finds me drifting in and out of consciousness, I wake up facing an enemy that I never wanted to meet; an enemy that continues to come towards me.

Uneasiness and insecurity originating from our government's insistence that we must travel this road in order to vanquish the evil in the other parts of the world, when in my subconscious mind I recognize that same evil to be present here at home. I can't dictate our country's foreign policy nor in any way make changes to that policy. I am a spectator on one hand, and a participant on the other. Perhaps not knowing the results of what actions we take as a nation is what concerns me the most.

The dreadfulness of watching the play unfold—knowing only too well that the outcome cannot be imagined. War is hell and lacks glory. There are no winners in war...only victims. Yet, to do nothing is to invite that continued sleeplessness and the marauding images that threaten our slumber. Has the world become so small and so crowded that all mankind co-habits an irritable state of existence? Is there nowhere on earth where people work together in finding solutions to shared problems? And have we become so menial in our interactions with others that the take-it-or-leave-it offer requires either acceptance or war?

There is too much immunity in our government. Our elected officials neither represent us, nor are cognizant of our humanitarian needs as a people. When faced with the situation of kill or be killed and the gut-wrenching reality that there are no other choices, our whole existence is degraded and hollowed. All that we have lived our lives for...becomes a mute matter. The last man standing still suffers death.

War wounds never heal—whether physical or mental. They are scars that provide a mending process but will always remain blemished. But scars, like war, are not necessary if our government of elected officials are diligent and steadfast in exerting their utmost effort in adverting war. Rarely do the instigators of war suffer—rather it is the common man who shoulders the arms, or the civilian whose life is forever altered by a government composed of strutting cocks in the chicken yard. Ego and bravado coupled with pride...and prejudice towards those who seek a peaceful solution.

Why must mankind destroy in order to build? I am an American. But I neither trust nor respect a government that continually formulates hidden agendas for the welfare of its people. I do not need nor want a government looking out for my welfare. And I do not want to see my country suffer needlessly because some heady and hierarchy bureaucrats think they can do a better job of running my life than what I can do for myself. What little freedom I do have…is mine alone.

And while I remain a free man I am willing to forgo the process of war and to work towards resolving possible conflict because, in my heart I know, once war is chosen as the only alternative, then there will be no further paths to travel.

Give peace a chance.

Causalities of War

The conflict within Iraq continues. Our troops, and those of our coalition, have taken casualties. What was once a blank chart now includes the columns of KIA (Killed in Action), WIA (Wounded in Action) and MIA (Missing in Action). In any war there are casualties. We would be naïve to think that this conflict would be any different. Like the beginnings of all conflicts there will always exist the spectator categories of the "Gung-Ho" and the "Doves".

As this conflict continues, we will find that these two categories will transform into perspectives that will continue to be altered by events as they occur, and will test the mettle of both. Both sides possess qualities worth consideration. However, both sides have one common denominator in that they lack the one key ingredient in this analysis of the war–personal sacrifice. While both categories may stress their adamancy and opinions, and even proclaim their intimacy with this conflict with reference to those loved ones directly involved in the fighting, neither side faces the minute-by-minute personal struggle of dodging the next bullet meant for them.

The Geneva Convention is a template for law-abiding countries and their fighting armies, especially regarding those who are captured by the enemy. Torture and executions are not condoned by the Geneva Convention. In the thick of war, prisoners are to be treated humanely. Prisoners are unarmed and pose no credible threat to the capturers. They should be "out of the war picture" but not out of mind. Certainly, they should not be a banner displayed by the country whose media seeks political and world-wide attention.

Without expounding upon the particulars, the basis of the Geneva Convention is simply that a country should treat prisoners of war the same as that country would want its prisoners treated. Since Iraq is not a law-abiding county in the international community we should not expect it to abide by the Geneva Convention, and therefore it should come as no surprise that any of our forces taken prisoners will be treated in accordance to those articles. Shock, disbelief and anger will follow as this conflict progresses.

War is a dirty business. Personal mistakes and tactical errors in the field further extend and compound the tragic scenes of combat. But when a conscious decision is made to torture and execute the prisoners of the opposing army, the rules of battle must be redrawn. Our democracy, which includes the media coverage, is in many instances our undoing. In reporting the atrocities to a democratic audience we are prevented and confined from taking appropriate counter action regarding the torture and execution of prisoners of war. If one side is bound by the Geneva Convention and the other side chooses to ignore those same articles, the real dilemma posed is not one of abidance but rather of reporting.

It would, therefore, be more prudent for the "Gung-Ho" and "Dove" categories to continue their debate of this war in their arena of non-participation and allow the actual combat units to continue in their arena of personal combat expertise. If torture and the execution of prisoners of war by the Iraqis are to be the norm for the day on the field of battle, then torture and the execution of prisoners of war should be the new rule for our troops as well. I am more than willing to look the other way.

Miles to Go Before I Sleep

Whose woods these are I think I know.
His house is in the village though;
He will not see me stopping here
To watch his woods fill up with snow.
My little horse must think it queer
To stop without a farmhouse near
Between the woods and frozen lake
The darkest evening of the year.
He gives his harness bells a shake
To ask if there is some mistake.
The only other sound's the sweep
Of easy wind and downy flake.
The woods are lovely, dark and deep.
But I have promises to keep,

And miles to go before I sleep,
And miles to go before I sleep

Robert Frost is one of my favorite poets. His poems bring comfort to me when the world that surrounds me is turbulent and chaotic. At times, too much of anything can be burdensome—like a nagging headache that won't go away. Aches and pains that make their residence in this body of mine. I'm tired. Tired of the same old expectations bearing the same old illusions that never come to be. I believe the malady is universally enhanced in that everyone suffers the same fate periodically.

Sometimes we just have to get away from it all and let the mind rest for awhile. Some folks seek a vacation in a far away land that offers exotic scenery. For others, perhaps an evening out for dining and relaxation. Other people prefer just spending a quiet evening at home, away from the daily congestion of traffic.

I enjoy the smell of moist pine needles on the ground and squirrels running through the branches overhead. Footsteps in a forest with little noise or trace. And everywhere I look, I encounter trees with branches laden with snow and a quietness that echoes my innermost thoughts. I can breathe the muskiness of the forest as perfume of a long ago love. And think of good things that I too often think little of. The sunshine beams its intensity into the synapses that have been conditioned to darkness, and every rock, limb and blade of dry brittle grass takes on a perspective of individuality, and yet, fits into this mosaic of nature. I know now that I needed to come here. The most uplifting part of this whole experience is that I no longer no why.

And miles to go before I sleep, And miles to go before I sleep.

A Good Day

It's a good day. Snow and thunder rolled into town yesterday afternoon and brought some enjoyable moisture that still lies upon the land. I had a great time enjoying my daughter's visit here in Cheyenne. I don't have to return to work until Monday evening. The air permeates with the glorious smell of humidity and lacks any presence of cordite.

The war is winding down and I can turn it off with the button on my remote. I had breakfast at Perkins Restaurant this morning that included a country omelet, hash browns, pancakes and coffee. No need to bathe my red pony because the village streets are all slop-covered and all the horses are wearing the same glistening grime. I had a restful night's sleep, in complete darkness, for a change.

There's nothing in the way of debts and I even have some extra "change" to burn. I'm enjoying hot showers that steam up the bathroom mirror again. Yes…it's a good day.

Later today, I'm going to cruise the city streets and stop in some shops and browse. I'll read the Sunday edition of the *Wyoming Tribune-Eagle* and catch up on the local village gossip. I'll devote a little time working on my website and cleaning up some files that need attention. Spring is officially here now, as is daylight savings time. I rolled my clocks forward because that's what civilization requires of me and I don't mind, because now I'm in sync with the rest of mankind. *The Complete Short Stories of Ernest Hemingway, The Finca Vigia Edition* beckons me to pick it up and begin reading once more where I last left off. And tonight I can stay up late and sleep in tomorrow morning. I'll call my son and daughter on my cell phone and converse with them for as long as I want with no airtime stipulations. Yes…it's a good day.

The beer is cold in the refrigerator. Grocery shopping is done for another week, as is the laundry. The apartment has been dusted and vacuumed. Boots have been cleaned and polished. There's no yard work to bother with, no livestock to feed, no outside chores, projects, or anything else on my agenda. It's my time, for the present. (I even let the maid take the day off, and the chauffer won't be required for awhile.) The only thing I'm lacking is a dog. I miss the canine accompaniment. With a dog, all that I have to do is to feed her, rub behind her ears, and play with her. Afterwards, she'll follow me anywhere. That's better than a spouse. (I sure didn't make any points with the female genre there!)

But what the heck, I'm enjoying bachelor life. I don't have to concern myself with personal appearance or trying to impress someone whose attention I desire. No need to worry about saying the "right" thing—no touchy-feely psychoanalysis and self-induced guilt trips. Nope—I can just be a guy. But I do miss the dog. I've dined out in restaurants three times in the last three days. No menus to prepare and no dishes afterwards. I've enjoyed talking with the other folks at the table while consuming the meals as well. I've bumped into my apartment neighbors a couple of times and got caught up on their life. The girl upstairs is due to deliver anytime now so soon I should hear baby sounds drifting downwards. And the man in her life is looking forward to becoming a proud papa.

It's easy to enjoy life's little things. Yes…it's a good day.

Far Away Land

Sweeping, panoramic, grass-swaying rolling hills with rocky outcrops and a blistering sun, baking the plains as far as the eye can see. Blue sky composed of white cumulus clouds throwing shadows across the landscape, and a dry, gentle breeze pulling moisture from every part of vegetation and body. Rough country that exudes extremism and compelling visions.

This part of Montana is rich in history and scenery. The interstate highway that lies to the west carrying its many travelers to unknown destinations bypasses this somber and scenic area, somehow even now; all of this remains remote and distant. At the entrance are the typical eating establishments and souvenir shops and parking lots filled with cars and trucks whose license plates tell where home is for many of those who have briefly paused in passing. What images and impressions will the casual observer take with them, and remember in the years to come?

Here remnants of history remain, from the rifle pits dug into the ground to the steep brush-covered crevices that etch downward to the river below where there are trees and shade, and where visitors are not allowed to travel. Watch your step—this is rattlesnake country. Stay on the paths and do not venture into the grassy areas. Signs posting a warning to the uninitiated. There is a small, scrubby bush just to the east of Reno Hill and beyond where one is allowed to walk.

Brown and tan hues intermingled with the fading green of the foliage, this vegetation stands sentinel upon this barren hill top, but carries the music of the Western Meadowlark. Plumage of yellow, gray and black, this bird's sweet musical lullaby is both uplifting and reflective of its surroundings. An orchestra with a single voice that captivates the listener's inner self. How can such a harsh land be the bosom and inspiration to such wildlife? This fragile existence that sings of beauty and oneness with the land and the sky above.

Walking slowly back along the path towards the monument, this picture of a moment in time will remain unchanged, forever locked away in memory. Where once a great battle raged and the screams and anguish of dying men filled the dust-laden air, now there is peace, and the song of the meadowlark. Old Glory flies proudly above this cemetery. Gusts of wind snap and crack the colors overhead, coupled with the low moaning sound of the pine needles and swaying branches, and shade that lends comfort from the heat out upon the plains.

Gravestones lie in the shadows with dates of departure to the early days of the frontier. There is no room left for any additional burials. Each marker a lasting testimonial to the departed veteran's soul. Truly, here is a final and peaceful bed for eternal slumber. What final price was exacted and under what circumstances no longer matters. That and the reality that just a short distance to the west the interstate highway whose travelers are mostly unaware of this tucked-away solitude.

What matters is that here was a story of a far away land, of soldiers fighting to stay alive, serving their time and duty to their nation, and finding a home where they sought none. Veterans sharing in death what they shared in life.

Here there are no bugles nor drums, or inspections or parades. Just the gentle breeze, and comforting shade, and in the distance...the meadowlark's song.

Computer Technology

I recall those days in the Army when I was a Captain and the "right-hand man" in the position of Executive Officer and Director of Support serving on the General Staff to the Commandant at Fort Harrison. We had several Army schools under our supervision then that included the Adjutant General Corps, Finance, Physical Fitness, Music, and Computer Science. I had to keep abreast of the latest information regarding the Army's intentions and its directions pertaining to each school.

During those days the "go-ahead" was given (financially and otherwise) for the Army to upgrade and to get in step with the rest of the world regarding computer technology. Many internal battles ensued regarding systems and technology, including the future outlook for their utilization. One of those issues involved the purchasing of computers and operating systems that could communicate with one another. Apple was in its infancy and IBM held the edge. (Microsoft was still in diapers.) Apple (later in adult life—Mac) lost any hope for being in compliance with the Army's needs. We must have done something correctly then, based upon the latest war results and the current computer technology that today's Army is utilizing. However, now it appears that the cart is before the horse, in that the military more often than not leads the way in incorporating that technology before the civilian market gets around to it. (And all of you thought we were just dumb "Grunts".)

This week, besides working my night job, I was involved with my own personal computers and their technology. This past Monday at three o'clock in the morning the spacebar on my Dell laptop computer stopped spacing. That particular feature has only to do one thing–space. And it couldn't do that. I ran several diagnostic tests on the system and came to the conclusion that it was definitely a hardware problem. I called the Dell Technical Support folks shortly thereafter, and after various questions from their technicians, they reached the same conclusion. "Around-the-clock" support and the keyboard didn't work. They told me to remove the hard drive and to send the laptop to them so they could replace the keyboard.

However, they forgot to notify Airborne Express. By Wednesday I called Dell at six o'clock in the morning and asked them where my courier was. Duh—they had not called. They also informed me that it could take up to ten days to get my laptop back to me again. So I followed their directions (and wrote a short letter to enclose with the laptop—with a few embellishments), removed the hard drive in sixty seconds (like hot-wiring a car) and I called Airborne Express shortly thereafter. Their courier soon showed up to whisk the laptop off to Dell for repairs.

There I was—naked without a computer. Not a pretty picture (in either instance). By Thursday afternoon (still naked and computer-less) I put on some clothes and went shopping and purchased a HP desktop system with all the bells and whistles—including a three year in-home service contract, the Windows XP operating system (like my Dell) and a DVD player/CD writer. And, it has a keyboard with a spacebar that works! I had just enough time to configure everything with the desktop system and to get it up and running before heading out to work Thursday evening. (I should still read the books that came with the computer when I get the time—but that's not important presently, because I have already done everything without the effort of reading beforehand.)

Anyway, Friday my Dell laptop was there at my door–repaired and ready to go again. I reinstalled the hard drive in thirty seconds (I'm getting better with age), booted it up—and everything worked. (Must have been something I said in my letter.) Since Friday, I've utilized my spare time reconfiguring both computer systems with updates in drivers and software so that I have compatibility between the laptop and the desktop. I've placed an order for a Direct Connect Cable and software from HP and it should arrive next week. So far, I've had to call the "around-the-clock" HP Technical Support folks a couple of times in the early morning hours ("oh-dark-thirty" Army time). One issue I had was that there were no driver and program software installation CD's with the system that I purchased. Not one CD! I was told by the Technical Support folks that HP does not include the CD's with the computers anymore because "the regular customer doesn't require them and besides, after a few years the customer can't figure out where they placed them anyway…" (I guess I'm not a "regular" customer though. HP is now sending me all of their CD's—free of charge, and they should arrive next week as well.)

While downloading the Windows XP updates from Microsoft last night I suddenly decided to go out for dinner at Shari's Restaurant. On the drive over there,

I popped in Celine Dion's "One Heart" CD (that gal can have my heart anytime she wants it!) into the red pony's CD player, cranked-up the volume, and recalled the days when the latest technology for the automobile was the eight-track player.

We've made some progress since then. The Army folded-up the horse cavalry at Fort Riley years ago (at any rate, I didn't see any horses while serving there) in the name of progress and technology—and went to machines instead. And in the name of progress and technology, I've now included on my outgoing emails which computer I actually utilized when working with Outlook Express. I really miss ranch life.

This hectic city life, weird work and sleeping schedules (that reminds me—I haven't had any sleep since noon Saturday, and here it is Sunday morning already), and the computer technology that constantly changes—what's this ol' country boy to do? Computers are just machines that need fine-tuning and adjustment periodically. And right now I'm tired of messing with them. Ah, what the hell…technology can wait. I'm going to a restaurant to eat breakfast…and I'll worry about technology and sleep later.

Last Verse

I started writing these *Considerations* a few years ago. Looking back, I realize now that what prompted me to do so was a certain amount of loneliness that had entered into my life. My wife had left my son and me and to go on the road for a year working for her employer and I began communicating my thoughts and observations to particular individuals by email. A marriage of twenty-three years is difficult to put aside, even when it's over.

People change, and sometimes they grow apart. So I took up the sport of writing. I call writing a "sport" because I was actively engaged in an activity that required a certain amount of concentration and degree of finesse, though I don't know that I've ever met that particular challenge in the opinion of my readers.

Each one of my *Considerations* was accomplished at one sitting–which is to say that I wrote what I felt at that particular moment without putting things on hold or into a draft format for further editing at a later date. The average time that I spent per writing was anywhere from thirty to forty-five minutes, and then it was gone forever out into the great void we call the internet.

I utilized a variety of computers other than my own depending upon where I was located at the time, and so I wish to thank those special individuals who allowed me access to their computer systems. Back in Indiana I wish to thank my sister Cheri Hovious and my sister-in-law Donna Jordan, and of course the Morgan County Public Library. My daughter Amanda Jordan and her fiancé Mike Kibbee of Westminster, Colorado who allowed me time on the computer at their home. And a special thanks to Mae Kirkbride and her daughter Barbie Crowl, both who gave me access to their computers so that I might remain in contact and continue sharing my thoughts with others while I was at the ranch.

My son Thomas will be arriving in Cheyenne later this morning to visit. I talked with him briefly yesterday afternoon prior to my departure for work again last night. (I've worked six nights this week, and now it is in the early hours of a Sunday morning and I'm tired and have not slept since the day before, but the mental process still goes on.) Thomas is moving to another apartment in Fort Collins, Colorado and no longer needs the computer system that I gave to him a year or so ago, and so he is returning it to dad. What will I do with three computer systems? Well, the one he is returning is the same one that I started writing my *Considerations* on a few years back. Like an old friend that one hasn't seen for awhile, it will be good to be reacquainted again. I learned a lot of computer stuff crashing that system and then fixing what I had done to it. (And now it's coming back for more.) More importantly, I'll get to share some time with my son.

"Sharing" is what I'd like to think that these writings have been about these last couple of years. Oh I know that I have been viewed as a devil's advocate, opinionated, preachy, and sarcastic, a social worker, a shrink, and even a medicine man. I've written about events in my life and the lives of others, and events going on in the world. I've shared my personal thoughts, observations, and "gut" feelings. In doing so, I've antagonized some of the same folks who in previous writings were nodding their heads and telling me that they agreed with me.

Complex, controversial, and creative—those three things have been the ideas that have wound my clock, and I hope wound your clock as well. It's what keeps us ticking. There comes a time when everyone should seek new challenges in their life.

"Challenge" is the oil that keeps the machinery running smoothly. Without the oil, everything eventually breaks down through neglect. And without challenge, life can become rather mundane. To those of you who in the past have provided me your thoughts and opinions regarding these writings–I thank you. And to the quiet observer who said nothing—you hold a special place in my heart as well. You see, each of us is special, in our own special way. If I have, in only one instance, created a reflective moment in your life, then you have thanked me for my efforts as well. There will be no further *Considerations*. The time has come to close this chapter in my life. That's not to say that I won't still be writing—it just means a different format is due and that the oil needs changing.

A special thanks to Gail Taylor, who I have chosen as my editor, and to whom I've never given ample opportunity to do her work. Gorgeous, you are a blessing! And for those of you that missed out on the earlier writings, one of these days...I'll get them into that book I've been promising. They might just be even better than they were when they were emails.

May in Wyoming is a special time of the year. The rains arrive; the grasses turn green, and the sage displaces an aroma that is unforgettable. It was in May thirty-five years ago that I first arrived here in this city they call Cheyenne, before heading on out to the ranch. A lot has happened in those intervening years.

Morning now...and the sun is seeking another new horizon, and this day is mine. I may not have the written words that you wanted to read, but you were there when the words needed thought. Besides the oil of challenge, there's also the grease of optimism. When the oil won't stay in place on the machinery, sometimes you just have to slop a little grease in its place instead.

The grease of optimism gives me hope, while the oil of challenge keeps me running. You've been good listeners—when I needed someone to listen. Good oil and good grease for this ol' boy. Thank you!

0-595-28346-2